You Have New Mail

Compiled by Earl Davison

First Edition – Published 2012

Published by : Earl Davison
978-0-9573811.

e-mail: earl.davison@ntlworld.com

Printed by:
Book Printing UK
Remus House
Coltsfoot Drive
Peterborough
Cambridgeshire
PE2 9JX
Tel: 017338980102
e-mail: info@bookprintinguk.com

GW00725934

For Amber & Thomas
With much love from Granddad

And with thoughts for our armed forces fighting for our
freedom.

I support 'Help for Heroes'.
If you wish to donate something please visit their website

www.helpforheroes.org.uk

Thank you

These are some of the many e-mails

received from friends and colleagues.

Mostly humorous, some informative,

others challenging, a few factual, a few stories
and

some others could make a tear come to your eye

All worth a read.

Sit back, relax, read and enjoy.

Acknowledgements

I am indebted to the many friends and colleagues that contributed to this book of e-mails.

Particular thanks go to Janice, Jim, Yvonne, Bob, Roy, Margaret, Mabel, Elaine, Kathy, Pete, Tony and to my wife Maureen for reading through the scripts and generally advising on suitability of material.

There are many, many e-mails that I just could not include due to the racial, religious, or sexual content. Great e-mails to some but quite unsuitable for public consumption.

e-mails are a great source of fun, knowledge, information and sometimes a great way to tax our minds.

Some of the e-mails you will have seen before, but, as I have found, it is great to read them again and again.

If you enjoy the book tell your friends.
If you didn't, or need some explanation of any of them, tell me, at

earl.davison@ntlworld.com

The book is written in UK English but includes e-mails from the USA, Canada and Australia as well as the UK

Subject: **FORREST GUMP GOES TO HEAVEN**

The day finally arrived. Forrest Gump dies and goes to Heaven.

He is at the Pearly Gates and met by St. Peter himself.

However, the gates are closed, and Forrest approaches the gatekeeper.

St. Peter says, 'Well, Forrest, it is certainly good to see you. I must tell you, though, that the place is filling up fast, and we have been administering an entrance examination for everyone.

The test is short, but you have to pass it before you can get into Heaven.'

Forrest responds, 'It sure is good to be here, St. Peter, sir.

But nobody ever told me about any entrance exam. I sure hope that the test ain't too hard.

Life was a big enough test as it was.'

St. Peter continued, 'Yes, I know, Forrest, but the test has only three questions.

First: - What two days of the week begin with the letter T?

Second: How many seconds are there in a year?

Third: What is God's first name?'

Forrest leaves to think the questions over.

He returns the next day and sees St. Peter, who waves him up, and says,

'Now that you have had a chance to think the questions over, tell me your answers.'

Forrest replies, 'Well, the first one – which two days in the week begins with the letter 'T'?

Shucks, that one is easy. That would be Today and Tomorrow.'

The Saint's eyes open wide and he exclaims, 'Forrest, that is not what I was thinking, but you do have a point, and I guess I did not specify, so I will give you credit for that answer. How about the next one?' asks St. Peter?

'How many seconds in a year? Now that one is harder,' replies Forrest, 'but I thunk and thunk about that, and I guess the only answer can be twelve.'

Astounded, St. Peter says, 'Twelve? Twelve? Forrest, how in Heaven's name could you come up with twelve seconds in a year?'

Forrest replies, 'Shucks, there's got to be twelve: January 2nd, February 2nd, March 2nd..'

'Hold it,' interrupts St. Peter. 'I see where you are going with this, and I see your point, though that was not quite what I had in mind... but I will have to give you credit for that one, too.

Let us go on with the third and final question.

Can you tell me God's first name'?

'Sure,' Forrest replies, 'its Andy.'

'Andy?' exclaims an exasperated and frustrated St Peter.

'Ok, I can understand how you came up with your answers to my first two questions, but just how in the world did you come up with the name Andy as God's first name?'

'Shucks, that was the easiest one of all,' Forrest replies. 'I learnt it from the song,

Andy Walks With Me,

Andy Talks With Me,

Andy Tells Me I Am His Own.'

St. Peter opened the Pearly Gates, and said: 'Run, Forrest, run.'

Subject: DID YOU HEAR

Got an e-mail today from a bored local housewife, 43, who was looking for some hot action!
So I sent her my ironing. That'll keep her busy.

Just had my water bill of £175 drop on my mat. That's a lot. Oxfam can supply a whole African village for just £2 a month. Time to change supplier me thinks.

Did you hear about the fat, alcoholic transvestite - All he wanted to do was eat, drink and be Mary.

After a night of drink, drugs and wild sex Bill woke up to find himself next to a really ugly woman. That's when he realised he had made it home safely.

Paddy says to Mick, "Christmas is on Friday this year".
Mick said, "Let's hope it's not the 13th then."

My mate just hired an Eastern European cleaner; took her 5 hours to hoover the house. Turns out she was a Slovak.

Since the snow came all the wife has done is look through the window. If it gets any worse, I'll have to let her in.

Came home today to find all my doors and windows smashed in and everything gone. What sort of sick person does that to someone's Advent calendar?

I've been charged with murder for killing a man with sandpaper. To be honest I only intended to rough him up a bit.

After years of research, scientists have discovered what makes women happy. - Nothing.

A lad comes home from school and excitedly tells his dad that he had a part in the school play and he was playing a man who had been married for 25 years. The dad says, "Never mind son, maybe next year you'll get a speaking part."

2 women called at my door and asked what bread I ate; when I said white, they gave me a lecture on the benefits of brown bread for 30 minutes. I think they were Hovis Witnesses.

A husband is someone who, after taking the trash out, gives the impression he just cleaned the whole house.

2

Subject Re: Why, Why, Why

Why do we press harder on a remote control when we know the batteries are getting dead?

Why do banks charge a fee on 'insufficient funds' when they know there is not enough money?

Why does someone believe you when you say there are four billion stars, but check when you say the paint is wet?

Why do they use sterilized needles for death by lethal injection?

Why doesn't Tarzan have a beard?

Why does Superman stop bullets with his chest, but ducks when you throw a revolver at him?

Why did Kamikaze pilots wear helmets?

Whose idea was it to put an 'S' in the word 'lisp'?

If people evolved from apes, why are there still apes?

Why is it that no matter what colour bubble bath you use the bubbles are always white?

Why do people constantly return to the refrigerator with hopes that something new to eat will have materialized?

Why do people keep running over a string a dozen times with their vacuum cleaner, then reach down, pick it up, examine it, then put it down to give the vacuum one more chance?

Why is it that no plastic bag will open from the end on your first try?

How do those dead bugs get into those enclosed light fixtures?

When we are in the supermarket and someone rams our ankle with a shopping cart then apologizes for doing so, why do we say, 'It's all right?' Well, it isn't all right, so why don't we say, 'That really hurt, why don't you watch where you're going?'

Why is it that whenever you attempt to catch something that's falling off the table you always manage to knock something else over?

In winter why do we try to keep the house as warm as it was in summer when we complained about the heat?

Why are there never any father-in-law jokes?

Did you hear about the fellow whose whole left side was cut off?
He's all right now.

Subject: SOME ONE LINERS

To write with a broken pencil is pointless.

A thief who stole a calendar got twelve months.

The batteries were given out free of charge.

A dentist and a manicurist married. They fought tooth and nail.

A boiled egg is hard to beat.

Police were called to a day care centre where a three-year-old was resisting a rest.

The guy who fell into an upholstery machine has now fully recovered.

He had a photographic memory which was never developed.

A will is a dead giveaway.

~~~~~~

Subject: Children's Logic:

"Give me a sentence about a public servant," said a teacher.
The small boy wrote:
"The fireman came down the ladder pregnant." The teacher took the lad aside to correct him. "Don't you know what pregnant means?" she asked.
"Sure," said the young boy confidently. "It means carrying a child."

~~~~~~

Subject: THOUGHT FOR THE DAY

A married man should forget his mistakes. There's no use in two people remembering the same thing!

~~~~~~

Subject: INDIAN TAXI DRIVERS

"A woman and her ten-year-old son were riding in a taxi in Mumbai.
It was raining and all the prostitutes were standing under the awnings.
"Mom," said the boy, "what are all those women doing?"
"They're waiting for their husbands to get off work," she replied.
The taxi driver turns around and says, "Geez lady, why don't you tell him the truth? They're hookers, boy! They have sex with men for money."
The little boy's eyes get wide and he says, "Is that true, Mom?" His mother, glaring hard at the driver, answers in the affirmative.
After a few minutes, the kid asks, "Mom, what happens to the babies those women have?"
"They become taxi drivers," she said."

Eagles may soar, but weasels don't get sucked into jet engines

4

Subject: THE AMBIDEXTROUS GOLFER

A group of 4 guys lived and died for their Saturday morning round of golf. One got transferred to another city. It wasn't the same without him.
A new woman joined their Club. She overheard the guys talking about their golf round. She said, "You know, I used to play on my golf team in college and I was pretty good. Would you mind if I joined you next week?"
The three guys looked at each other. Not one of them wanted to say 'yes', but she had them on the spot. Finally, one man said it would be okay, but they would be starting early - at 6:30 a.m. He figured the early tee-time would discourage her.
The woman said this may be a problem, and asked if she could be up to 15 minutes late. They rolled their eyes, but said okay. She smiled and said, "Good, I'll be there at 6:30 or 6:45."
She showed up at 6:30 sharp, and, playing right-handed, beat all three of them with an eye-opening two-under-par. She was fun and a pleasant person, and the guys were impressed. Back at the clubhouse, they congratulated her and invited her back the next week. She smiled, and said, "I'll be there at 6:30 or 6:45."
The next week she again showed up at 6:30 sharp. Only this time, she played left-handed. The three guys were incredulous as she still beat them with an even par round, despite playing with her off-hand. They were totally amazed. They couldn't figure her out. She was again very pleasant and didn't seem to be purposely showing them up. They invited her back again, but each man harboured a burning desire to beat her.
The third week, the guys had their game faces on. But this time, she was 15 minutes late, which made the guys irritable. This week the lady again played right-handed, and narrowly beat all of them. The men mused that her late arrival was due to petty gamesmanship on her part. However, she was so gracious and so complimentary of their play, they couldn't hold a grudge. Back in the clubhouse, all three guys were shaking their heads. This woman was a riddle no one could figure out. They had a couple of beers, and finally, the men asked her point blank, "How do you decide if you're going to golf right-handed or left handed?"
The lady blushed, and grinned. "That's easy," she said. "When my Dad taught me to play golf, I learned I was ambidextrous. I like to switch back and forth. When I got married after college, I discovered my husband always sleeps in the nude. From then on, I developed a silly habit. Right before I left in the morning for golf practice, I would pull the covers off him. If his, you-know-what, was pointing to the right, I golfed right-handed; if it was pointed to the left, I golfed left-handed."
The guys thought this was hysterical. Astonished at this bizarre information, one of the guys shot back, "But what if it's pointing straight up?"

She said, "Then, I'm fifteen minutes late."

Subject: At a Budapest zoo:

Please do not feed the animals. If you have any suitable food, give it to the guard on duty.

~~~~~~

Subject: THIS ONE REALLY TOUCHED MY HEART

"Dear God, this year please send clothes for all those poor ladies in Daddy's computer",
Amen.

~~~~~~

Where does Grandma Live

A 6-year-old was asked where his grandma lived. "Oh," he said, "she lives at the airport, and when we want her, we just go get her. Then, when we're done having her visit, we take her back to the airport."

~~~~~~

Subject: PADDY MURPHY

Into a Belfast pub comes Paddy Murphy, looking like he'd just been run over by a train. His arm is in a sling, his nose is broken, his face is cut and bruised and he's walking with a limp.
"What happened to you?" asks Sean the bartender.
"Jamie O'Conner and me had a fight," says Paddy.
"That *little* O'Conner," says Sean, "He couldn't do that to you, he must have had something in his hand."
"That he did," says Paddy," a shovel is what he had and a terrible lickin' he gave me with it."
"Well," says Sean, "you should have defended yourself, didn't you have something in your hand?"
"That I did," said Paddy..."Mrs. O'Conner's breast, and a thing of beauty it was, but useless in a fight."

~~~~~~

Subject: Get me a parking place

Paddy was driving down the street in a sweat because he had an important meeting and couldn't find a parking place. Looking up to heaven he said, 'Lord take pity on me. If you find me a parking place I will go to Mass every Sunday for the rest of my life and give up me Irish whiskey!'
Miraculously, a parking place appeared.
Paddy looked up again and said, 'Never mind, I found one.'

~~~~~~

The liquid inside young coconuts can be used as a substitute for Blood plasma.

~~~~~~

Paddy's in the bathroom and Murphy shouts to him. "Did you find the shampoo?" Paddy says, "yes but it's for dry hair and I've just wet mine."

6

Subject: DID YOU HEAR 2

I went to the cemetery yesterday to lay some flowers on a grave. As I was standing there I noticed 4 grave diggers walking about with a coffin, 3 hours later and they're still walking about with it. **I thought to myself, they've lost the plot!!**

My daughter asked me for a pet spider for her birthday, so I went to our local pet shop and they were £70!!!
Stuff that, I thought, I can get one cheaper off the web.

Statistically, 6 out of 7 dwarves are not happy.

I was walking in a cemetery this morning and saw a bloke hiding behind a gravestone. "Morning." I said. "No" he replied, "just having a pee."

I start a new job in Seoul next week. I thought it was a good Korea move.

I was driving this morning when I saw an RAC breakdown van parked up. The driver was sobbing uncontrollably and looked very miserable.
I thought to myself 'that guy's heading for a breakdown'.

Subject: CONFESSION

A bride on her wedding night says to her husband 'I must confess darling, I was a hooker[1]!'

He says 'That's all right, dear. Your past is your past, but I must admit that I find it quite erotic. Tell me about it'.

She replies 'Well, my name was Nigel, and I played for Wigan!'

~~~~~~

```
The first owner of the Marlboro Company died of lung cancer.
So did the first 'Marlboro Man'.
```

~~~~~~

A man rang the Incontinence Hotline.
They said **"Can you hold please"**

The early bird gets the worm, but the second mouse gets the cheese

Coca-Cola was originally green.

7

Subject: Aging

A group of 40-year-old girlfriends discussed where they should meet for dinner. Finally, it was agreed that they should meet at the Ocean View restaurant because the waiters there had tight pants and nice bums.

10 years later at 50 years of age, the group once again discussed where they should meet for dinner. Finally, it was agreed that they should meet at the Ocean View restaurant because the food there was very good and the wine selection was excellent.

10 years later at 60 years of age, the group once again discussed where they should meet for dinner. Finally, it was agreed that they should meet at the Ocean View restaurant because they could eat there in peace and quiet and the restaurant had a beautiful view of the ocean.

10 years later, at 70 years of age, the group once again discussed where they should meet for dinner. Finally, it was agreed that they should meet at the Ocean View restaurant because the restaurant was wheel chair accessible and they even had an elevator.

10 years later, at 80 years of age, the group once again discussed where they should meet for dinner. Finally, it was agreed that they should meet at the Ocean View restaurant because they had never been there before.

Subject: THE BIG BIKER

There I was is sitting at the bar staring at my drink when a really big, trouble-making biker steps up next to me, grabs my drink and gulps it down in one swig. "Well, whatcha gonna do about it?" he says, menacingly, as I burst into tears. "Come on, man," the biker says, "I didn't think you'd CRY. I can't stand to see a man crying."

"This is the worst day of my life," I say. "I'm a complete failure. I was late to a meeting and my boss fired me. When I went to the parking lot, I found my car had been stolen and I don't have any insurance. I left my wallet in the cab I took home. I found my old lady in bed with the gardener, and then my dog bit me."

"So I came to this bar to work up the courage to put an end to it all. I buy a drink; I drop a capsule in and sit here watching the poison dissolve. Then you, you asshole, show up and drink the whole thing! But enough about me, how's your day going?"

A spa hotel is like a normal hotel, only in reception there's a picture of a pebble.

Man who wants pretty nurse, must be patient

8

Subject: **The price of Petrol versus Printer Ink**

All these examples do NOT imply that petrol is cheap; it just illustrates how outrageous some prices are....
You will be really shocked by the last one!
(At least, I was...)
Compared with Petrol......
Think a gallon of petrol is expensive?
This makes one think, and also puts things in perspective.

Tippex 7 oz £1.39 ....£5.42 per gallon
Lipton Ice Tea 16 oz £1.19 ....£9.52 per gallon
Ocean Spray 16 oz £1.25 .... £10.00 per gallon
Evian water 9 oz £1.49................ £21.19 per gallon!
 £21.19 for WATER and the buyers don't even know the source
(Evian spelled backwards is Naive.)
Brake Fluid 12 oz £3.15 .... £33.60 per gallon
Vick's Nyquil 6 oz £8.35 .... £178.13 per gallon
Ever wonder why printers are so cheap?
So they have you hooked for the ink.
The cost of the ink comes out about £2,270 a gallon!!!
Chanel No 5 (£51.60 for one 3.4 ounce bottle). £2,430 per gallon!!!!!!!!!
So, the next time you're at the pump be glad your car doesn't run on Water, Tippex, Printer Ink or God forbid, perfume!!!!
Just a little humour to help ease the pain of your next trip to the petrol pump.

:::

A duck's quack doesn't echo, and no one knows why.

:::

A Sunday school teacher was discussing the Ten Commandments with her five and six year olds.
After explaining the commandment to 'honour' thy Father and thy Mother, she asked, 'Is there a commandment that teaches us how to treat our brothers and sisters?'
From the back, one little boy (the oldest of a family) answered, 'Thou shall not kill.'

You don't stop laughing because you grow old.
You grow old because you stop laughing

9

Subject: THE DIFFERENCE IF YOU MARRY AN ULSTER GIRL

Three friends married women from different parts of the UK.
The first man married a woman from Wales. He told her that she was to do the dishes and house cleaning. It took a couple of days, but on the third day, he came home to see a clean house and dishes washed and put away.
The second man married a woman from England. He gave his wife orders that she was to do all the cleaning, dishes and the cooking. The first day he didn't see any results, but the next day he saw it was better. By the third day, he saw his house was clean, the dishes were done, and there was a huge dinner on the table.
The third man married a girl from Ulster. He ordered her to keep the house cleaned, dishes washed, lawn mowed, laundry washed, and hot meals on the table for every meal. He said the first day he didn't see any improvement, the second day he didn't see anything but by the third day, some of the swelling had gone down and he could see a little out of his left eye, and his arm was healed enough that he could fix himself a sandwich and load the dishwasher. He still has some difficulty when he pees.

Subject: Hot and Cold sex

After an examination, the doctor said to his elderly patient: 'You appear to be in good health. Do you have any medical concerns you would like to ask me about?'
In fact, I do.' said the old man. "After my wife and I have sex, I'm usually cold and chilly; and then, after I have sex with her the second time, I'm usually hot and sweaty."
When the doctor examined his elderly wife a short time later he said, 'everything appears to be fine. Are there any medical concerns that you would like to discuss with me?'
The lady replied that she had no questions or concerns. The doctor then said to her: 'Your husband mentioned an unusual problem. He claimed that he was usually cold and chilly after having sex with you the first time; and then hot and sweaty after the second time. Do you have any idea about why?'
'Oh, that crazy old bastard' she replied. 'That's because the first time is usually in January, and the second time is in July."

Subject: "Jesus Knows you're here"

A burglar broke into a house one night.

He shined his flashlight around, looking for valuables when a voice in the dark said,

'Jesus knows you're here.'

He nearly jumped out of his skin, clicked his flashlight off, and froze.

When he heard nothing more, after a bit, he shook his head and continued.

Just as he pulled the stereo out so he could disconnect the wires, clear as a bell he heard   'Jesus is watching you.'

Freaked out, he shined his light around frantically, looking for the source of the voice.

Finally, in the corner of the room, his flashlight beam came to rest on a parrot.

'Did you say that?' he hissed at the parrot.

'Yep', the parrot confessed, then squawked, 'I'm just trying to warn you, Jesus is watching you.'

The burglar relaxed. 'Warn me, huh? Who in the world are you?'

'Moses,' replied the bird.

'Moses?' the burglar laughed.

'What kind of people would name a bird Moses?'

'The kind of people that would name a Rottweiler Jesus.'

Subject: "Morning Sex"

She was standing in the kitchen, preparing our usual soft-boiled eggs and toast for breakfast, wearing only the 'T' shirt that she normally slept in.

As I walked in, almost awake, she turned to me and said softly, "You've got to make love to me this very moment!"

My eyes lit up and I thought, "I am either still dreaming or this is going to be my lucky day!"

Not wanting to lose the moment, I embraced her and then gave it my all; right there on the kitchen table.

Afterwards she said, "Thanks," and returned to the stove, her T-shirt still around her neck.

Happy, but a little puzzled, I asked,

"What was that all about?"

She explained, "The egg timer's broken."

If you want your spouse to listen and pay strict attention to every word you say, talk in your sleep.

Subject: Air Travel

A guy is sitting in the bar in departures at Heathrow. A beautiful woman walks in and sits down at the table next to him.

He decides because she's got a uniform on, she's probably an off duty flight attendant.

So he decides to have a go at picking her up by identifying the airline she flies for thereby impressing her greatly.

He leans across to her and says the Delta Airlines motto: "We love to fly and it shows ".

The woman looks at him blankly.

He sits back and thinks up another line.

He leans forward again and delivers the Air France motto: "Winning the hearts of the world".

Again she just stares at him with a slightly puzzled look on her face.

Undeterred, he tries again, this time saying the Malaysian Airlines motto: "Going beyond expectations".

The woman looks at him sternly and says;" What the f**k do you want?"

"Ah!" he says, sitting back with a smile on his face, "Ryanair[2]"

Subject: Snow White & the Seven Dwarfs.

The seven dwarfs always left to go work in the mine early each morning.
As always, Snow White stayed home doing her domestic chores.
As lunchtime approached, she would prepare their lunch and carry it to the mine.
One day as she arrived at the mine with the lunch, she saw that there had been a terrible cave-in.
Tearfully, and fearing the worst, Snow White began calling out, hoping against hope that the dwarfs had somehow survived.
'Hello...Hello!' she shouted. 'Can anyone hear me? Hello!'
For a long while, there was no answer. Losing hope, Snow White again shouted, 'Hello! Is anyone down there?'
Just as she was about to give up all hope, she heard a faint voice from deep within the mine, singing;
ENGLAND FOR THE WORLD CUP
Snow White fell to her knees and prayed, 'Oh, thank you, God!
At least Dopey is still alive.'

A lion will not cheat on his wife, but a Tiger Would!

I may be Schizophrenic, but at least I have each other.

Subject: Men Are Just Happier People

NICKNAMES
If Laura, Kate and Sarah go out for lunch, they call each other Laura, Kate and Sarah. If Mike, Dave and John go out, they will affectionately refer to each other as Fat Boy, Dickhead and Shit for Brains.

EATING OUT
When the bill arrives, Mike, Dave and John will each throw in £20, even though it's only for £32.50. None will actually admit they want change back.
When the girls get their bill, out come the pocket calculators.

MONEY
A man will pay £2 for a £1 item he needs.
A woman will pay £1 for a £2 item that she doesn't need but it's on sale.

BATHROOMS
A man has six items in his bathroom: toothbrush and toothpaste, shaving cream, razor, shower gel, and a towel.
The average number of items in the typical woman's bathroom is 337.
A man would not be able to identify more than 10 of these items.

ARGUMENTS
A woman has the last word in any argument.
Anything a man says after that is the beginning of a new argument.

FUTURE
A woman worries about the future until she gets a husband.
A man never worries about the future until he gets a wife.

SUCCESS
A successful man is one who makes more money than his wife can spend.
A successful woman is one who can find such a man.

MARRIAGE
A woman marries a man expecting he will change, but he doesn't.
A man marries a woman expecting that she won't change, but she does.

DRESSING UP
A woman will dress up to go shopping, water the plants, empty the trash, answer the phone, read a book, and get the mail.
A man will dress up for weddings and funerals.

NATURAL
Men wake up as good-looking as they went to bed. Women somehow deteriorate during the night.

OFFSPRING
Ah, children. A woman knows all about her children.
She knows about dentist appointments and romances, birthdays, best friends, favourite foods, shoe sizes, clothes, secret fears and hopes and dreams.
A man is vaguely aware of some small people living in the house.

Woman who live in glass house should change clothes in basement.

Subject: ASK AND IT SHALL BE GIVEN

The minister was preoccupied with thoughts of how he was going to ask the congregation to come up with more money than they were expecting for repairs to the church building. Therefore, he was annoyed to find that the regular organist was sick and a substitute had been brought in at the last minute. The substitute wanted to know what to play.

"Here's a copy of the service," he said impatiently. "But, you'll have to think of something to play after I make the announcement about the finances."

During the service, the minister paused and said, "Brothers and Sisters, we are in great difficulty; the roof repairs cost twice as much as we expected and we need $4,000 more. Any of you who can pledge $100 or more, please stand up."

At that moment, the substitute organist played "The Star Spangled Banner."

And that is how the substitute became the regular organist!

Subject: The Silent Treatment

A man and his wife were having some problems at home and were giving each other the silent treatment.

Suddenly, the man realized that the next day, he would need his wife to wake him at 5:00 AM for an early morning business flight.

Not wanting to be the first to break the silence (and LOSE), he wrote on a piece of paper,

'Please wake me at 5:00 AM.' He left it where he knew she would find it.

The next morning, the man woke up, only to discover it was 9:00 AM and he had missed his flight

Furious, he was about to go and see why his wife hadn't wakened him, when he noticed a piece of paper by the bed.

The paper said, 'It is 5:00 AM. Wake up. .'

Men are not equipped for these kinds of contests.

No piece of paper can be folded in half more than seven (7) times. OK go ahead...I'll wait...

Subject: SENIOR DATING

Dorothy and Edna, two "senior" widows, are talking.

Dorothy: "That nice George Johnson asked me out for a date. I know you went out with him last week, and I wanted to talk with you about him before I give him my answer."

Edna: "Well, I'll tell you. He shows up at my apartment punctually at 7 p.m., dressed like such a gentleman in a fine suit, and he brings me such beautiful flowers! Then he takes me downstairs, and what's there but a luxury car, a limousine, uniformed chauffeur and all. Then he takes me out for dinner... a marvellous dinner... lobster, champagne, dessert, and after-dinner drinks. Then we go see a show. Let me tell you, Dorothy, I enjoyed it so much I could have just died from pleasure!

So then we are coming back to my apartment and he turns into an ANIMAL. Completely crazy, he tears off my expensive new dress and has his way with me two times!"

Dorothy: "Goodness gracious! So you are telling me I shouldn't go out with him?"

Edna: "No, no, no... I'm just saying, wear an old dress

Subject: Prescription Drugs and Side Effects

A woman asks her husband at breakfast time, "Would you like some bacon and eggs, a slice of toast, and maybe some grapefruit juice and coffee?" He declines. "Thanks for asking, but I'm not hungry right now. It's this Viagra," he says. "It's really taken the edge off my appetite."

At lunchtime, she asked him if he would like something. "How about a bowl of soup, homemade muffins, or a cheese sandwich?" He declines. "The Viagra," he says, "really trashes my desire for food."

Come dinnertime, she asks if he wants anything to eat. "Would you like a juicy rib eye steak and some scrumptious apple pie? Or maybe a rotisserie chicken or tasty stir fry?" He declines again. "No, "he says, "it's got to be the Viagra. I'm still not hungry."

"Well," she says, "Would you mind letting me up? I'm starving."

Subject: Remember this motto to live by:

Life should NOT be a journey to the grave with the intention of arriving safely in an attractive and well preserved body, but rather to skid in sideways, chocolate in one hand, wine in the other, body thoroughly used up, totally worn out and screaming 'WOO HOO what a ride!'

A bank is a place that will lend you money, if you can prove that you don't need it.

OLD ACTORS never die, they just drop a part

Subject: How Old Is Grandma?

One evening a grandson was talking to his grandmother about current events. The grandson asked his grandmother what she thought about the schools, the computer age, and just things in general.

The Grandma replied, "Well, let me think a minute,

I was born before: television, polio shots, frozen foods, Xerox, contact lenses, Frisbees and the pill.

There was no: credit cards, laser beams or ball-point pens.

Man had not invented: pantyhose, air conditioners, dishwashers, clothes dryers, and the clothes were hung out to dry in the fresh air and man hadn't yet walked on the moon.

Your Grandfather and I got married first-and then lived together.

Every family had a father and a mother.

Until I was 25, I called every man, older than I, 'Sir'

We were before gay-rights and computer- dating,

We were taught to know the difference between right and wrong and to stand up and take responsibility for our actions.

Living in and serving your country was a privilege;

We thought fast food was what people ate during Lent.

Having a meaningful relationship meant getting along with your cousins.

Draft dodgers were people who closed their front doors when the evening breeze started.

Time-sharing meant time the family spent time together -not buying villas.

We never heard of FM radios, tape decks, iPods, CDs, DVD's, computers, electric typewriters, yogurt, or guys wearing earrings.

If you saw anything with 'Made in Japan ' on it, it was junk.

The term 'making out' referred to how you did on your school exam.

Pizza Hut, McDonald's, and instant coffee were unheard of. Ice-cream cones, phone calls, rides on a streetcar, and a Pepsi were all a nickel.

You could buy a new Chevy Coupe for $600 but who could afford one? Too bad, because gas was 11 cents a gallon.

In my day: "grass" was mowed, "coke" was a drink, "pot" was something your mother cooked in and "rock music" was your grandmother's lullaby.

"chip" meant a piece of wood, "hardware" was found in a hardware store and "software" wasn't even a word.

Now here is the shock people call us "old

This Woman could be only 58 years old today!!!!!!!!

Subject: If Only!!!!

The Liverpool' football manager flew to Bagdad to watch a young Iraqi play football and is suitably impressed and arranges him to come over to Anfield. Two weeks later Liverpool are 4-0 down to Manchester Utd with only 20 minutes left to play. The manager gives the young Iraqi striker the nod and on he goes. The lad is a sensation, scores 5 goals in 20 minutes and wins the game for Liverpool.

The fans are delighted, the players and coaches are delighted and the media love this new star.

When the player comes off the pitch he phones his mum to tell her about his first day in English football.

'Hello mum, guess what?' he says 'I played for 20 minutes today, and we were 4-0 down but I scored 5 and we won. Everybody loves me, the fans, the media, they all love me.'

'Wonderful,' says his mum, 'Let me tell you about my day. Your father got shot in the street and robbed; your sister and I were ambushed, gang raped and beaten and your brother has joined a gang of looters and all the while you were having such a great time playing bloody football.'

The young lad is very upset. 'What can I say mum, but I'm so sorry.'

Sorry?!!! Sorry?!!!' shrieks his mum, It's your bloody fault we moved to Liverpool in the first Place.

Subject: Words ending in tor

A teacher asks the class to name things that end with 'tor' that eat things.
The first little boy says, "Alligator."
"Very good, that's a big word."
The second boy says, "Predator."
"Yes, that's another big word. Well done."
The third boy says, "Vibrator, Miss."
After nearly falling off her chair, she says, "That is a big word, but it doesn't eat anything."
"Well my sister has one and she says it eats batteries like there's no tomorrow!

Subject: Venus

Venus is the only planet that rotates clockwise.
(Since Venus is normally associated with women, what does this tell you?)
(That women are going in the 'right' direction?)

Subject: WOMEN'S REVENGE

'Cash, check or charge?' I asked, after folding items the woman wished to purchase.

As she fumbled for her wallet, I noticed a remote control for a television set in her purse.

'So, do you always carry your TV remote?' I asked.

'No,' she replied, 'but my husband refused to come shopping with me, and I figured this was the most evil thing I could do to him legally.'

Subject: An Irishman is cleaning his rifle and accidentally shoots his wife.

He immediately dials 999.

Irishman: *"It's my fooken wife! I've accidentally shot her, I've fooken killed her!"*

Operator: *"Please calm down Sir. Can you first make sure she is actually dead!"*

click .... *BANG*

Irishman: *"Okay, I've fooken done that. What next ?"*

Subject: HARRODS

A lady walks into Harrods[4]. She looks around, spots a beautiful diamond bracelet and walks over to inspect it. As she bends over to look more closely, she unexpectedly farts.

Very embarrassed, she looks around nervously to see if anyone noticed her little woops and prays that a sales person was not anywhere near.

As she turns around, her worst nightmare materializes in the form of a salesman standing right behind her - Good looking as well!

Cool as a cucumber, he displays all of the qualities one would expect of a professional in a store like Harrods.

He politely greets the lady with, 'Good day, Madam. How may we help you today?

Blushing and uncomfortable, but still hoping that the salesman somehow missed her little 'incident', she asks, 'Sir, what is the price of this lovely bracelet?'

He answers,

"Madam - if you farted just looking at it - you're going to s**t yourself when I tell you the price!"

Subject: THE POPE COMES TO GLASGOW

The Pope comes to Glasgow and asks "Anyone with 'special needs' who wants to be prayed over, please come forward to the front by the altar."

With that, wee Brendon got in line, and when it was his turn, the Pope asked, "My son, what do you want me to pray about for you?"

Wee Brendon replied, "Your Holiness, I need you to pray for help with my hearing."

The Pope put one finger in Brendon's ear, placed his other hand on top of his head, and then prayed and prayed and prayed. He prayed a great prayer for Brendon, and the whole congregation joined in with great enthusiasm.

After a few minutes, the Pope removed his hands, stood back and asked, "Brendon how is your hearing now?"

Wee Brendon answered, "Ah don't know. It's no' 'til Tuesday next week....."

Subject: Irish Pick-up line!

An Irishman walks into a pub and takes a seat next to a very attractive woman.

He gives her a quick glance then casually looks at his watch for a moment.

The woman notices this and asks, 'Is your date late?'

'No', he replies, 'I just got this state-of the-art watch, and I was just testing it.'

The intrigued woman says, 'a state-of-the-art watch? ''What's so special about it?'

The Irishman explains, 'It uses alpha waves to talk to me telepathically.'

The lady says, 'What's it telling you now?'

'Well, it says you're not wearing any knickers.'

The woman giggles and replies 'Well it must be broken because I am wearing knickers!'

The Irishman smiles, taps his watch and says, 'Bloody thing's an hour fast!'

The statistics on sanity is that one out of every four persons is suffering from some sort of mental illness. Think of your three best friends -- if they're okay, then it's you.

Drink 'till she's cute, but stop before the wedding

Subject: Paddy's lawn

Paddy was waiting at the bus stop with his mate when a lorry went by loaded up with rolls of turf.
Paddy said, 'I gonna do that when I win the lottery'
'What's dat, says his mate.
'Send me lawn away to be cut'.

Subject: Sweet Tea

A woman goes to the doctor, beaten black and Blue.
Doctor: "What happened?"
Woman: "Doctor, I don't know what to do. Every time my husband comes home drunk he beats me to a pulp."
Doctor: "I have a real good cure for that. When your husband comes home drunk, just take a glass of sweet tea and start swishing it in your mouth. Just swish and swish but don't swallow until he goes to bed and is asleep."
Two weeks later the woman comes back to the doctor looking fresh and reborn.
Woman: "Doctor that was a brilliant idea! Every time my husband came home drunk, I swished with sweet tea. I swished and swished, and he didn't touch me!"
Doctor: "You see how keeping your mouth shut helps?"

Subject: THE FUNERAL

A man was leaving a convenience store with his morning coffee when he noticed a most unusual funeral procession approaching the nearby cemetery. A long black hearse was followed by a second long black hearse about 50 feet behind the first one. Behind the second hearse was a solitary man walking a dog on a leash. Behind him, a short distance back, were about 200 men walking single file. The man couldn't stand the curiosity. He respectfully approached the man walking the dog and said, "I am so sorry for your loss, and this may be a bad time to disturb you, but I've never seen a funeral like this..."Whose funeral is it?"   "My wife's."
"What happened to her?"
The man replied, "My dog attacked and killed her."
He inquired further, "But who is in the second hearse?"
The man answered, "My mother-in-law. She was trying to help my wife when the dog turned on her and killed her too."
A very poignant and touching moment, of brotherhood and silence, passed between the two men.
"Can I borrow the dog?"
The man replied, "Get in line."

Subject: SNOW FALL

This had most of the state of Michigan in America laughing for 2 days and a very embarrassed female news anchor who will, in the future, think before she speaks.

What happens when you predict snow but don't get any!

We had a female news anchor, the day after it was supposed to have snowed and didn't, turned to the weatherman and asked:

"So Bob, where's that 8 inches you promised me last night?"

Not only did he have to leave the set, but half the crew did too.!

Subject: THE SPEECH THERAPIST

In the U.K., a very pretty young speech therapist was getting nowhere with her "Stammerers Action Group". She had tried every technique in the book without the slightest success. No-one was improving. Finally, thoroughly exasperated, she said "If any of you can tell me, without stuttering, the name of the town where you were born I will have wild and passionate sex with you until your muscles ache and your eyes water.

So, who wants to go first?"

The Englishman piped up.

"B-b-b-b-b-b-b-irmingham."

"That's no use, Trevor," said the speech therapist. "Who's next?"

The Scotsman raised his hand and blurted out

"P-p-p-p-p-p-p-p-aisley".

"That's no better.

There'll be no sex for you, I'm afraid, Hamish."

"How about you, Paddy?"

The Irishman took a deep breath and eventually blurted out " London ."

"Brilliant, Paddy!" said the speech therapist and immediately set about living up to her promise.

After 15 minutes of exceptionally steamy sex, the couple paused for breath and Paddy said

"-d-d-d-d-d-d-d-d-erry".

When everything's coming your way, you're in the wrong lane.

Women would rather have beauty than brains because the average man can see better than he can think.

Subject: Doctor's office, Rome :

SPECIALIST IN WOMEN AND OTHER DISEASES.

Subject: **MICROSOFT Vs GENERAL MOTORS**

At a recent computer expo (COMDEX), Bill Gates reportedly compared the computer industry with the auto industry and stated,

'If GM had kept up with technology like the computer industry has, we would all be driving cars that got 1,000 miles to the gallon.'

In response to Bill's comments, General Motors issued a press release stating:

If GM had developed technology like Microsoft, we would all be driving cars with the following characteristics

1.   For no reason whatsoever, your car would crash ... twice a day.

2.   Every time they repainted the lines in the road, you would have to buy a new car.

3.   Occasionally your car would die on the freeway for no reason. You would have to pull to the side of the road, close all of the windows, shut off the car, restart it, and reopen the windows before you could continue. For some reason you would simply accept this.

4.   Occasionally, executing a manoeuvre such as a left turn would cause your car to shut down and refuse to restart, in which case you would have to reinstall the engine.

5.   Macintosh would make a car that was powered by the sun, was reliable, five times as fast and twice as easy to drive - but would run on only five percent of the roads.

6.   The oil, water temperature and alternator warning lights would all be replaced by a single 'This Car Has Performed An Illegal Operation' warning light.

7.   The airbag system would ask 'Are you sure?' before deploying.

8.   Occasionally, for no reason, your car would lock you out and refuse to let you in until you simultaneously lifted the door handle, turned the key and grabbed hold of the radio antenna.

9.   Every time a new car was introduced, car buyers would have to learn how to drive all over again because none of the controls would operate in the same manner as the old car.

10. You'd have to press the 'Start' button to turn the engine off.

PS: I 'd like to add that when all else fails, you could call 'customer service' in some foreign country and be instructed in some foreign language how to fix your car yourself!!!!

Subject: THE CHALLENGED HUSBAND

One day my housework-challenged husband decided to wash
his sweatshirt Seconds after he stepped into the
laundry room, he shouted to me, "What setting do I use
on the washing machine?"
"It depends," I replied. "What does it say on your
shirt?"
He yelled back, "BUDWEISER."
And they say blondes are dumb...

Subject: THE SPEEDING SENIOR CITIZEN

A senior citizen drove his brand new corvette convertible out of the
dealership....taking off down the road, he floored it to 80 mph, enjoying the
wind blowing through what little hair he had left.
"Amazing," he thought as he flew down the highway, pushing the pedal
even more. Looking in his rear view mirror, he saw a state trooper behind
him, lights flashing and siren blaring. He floored it to 100 mph, then 110.
Suddenly he thought, "What am I doing?
I'm too old for this," and pulled over to await the trooper's arrival.
The trooper walked up to the corvette, looked at his watch and said, "Sir,
my shift ends in 30 minutes, today is Friday. If you can give me a reason for
speeding that I've never heard before, I'll let you go."
The old gentleman paused. Then said, "years ago, my wife ran off with a
state trooper, I thought you were bringing her back."
"Have a good day, sir, " replied the trooper.

Subject: THE DENTIST

A guy and a girl meet at a bar. They get along so well that they decide to go to the
girl's place.
A few drinks later, the guy takes off his shirt and then washes his hands.
He then takes off his trousers and again washes his hands.
The girl has been watching him and says: 'You must be a dentist.'
The guy, surprised, says: 'Yes .... How did you figure that out?'
'Easy.' she replies, 'you keep washing your hands.'
One thing leads to another and they make love.
After it's over the girl says: 'You must be a *good* dentist.'
The guy, now with an inflated ego, says: 'Sure - I'm a good dentist.
How did you figure that out?'
The girl replies: 'Didn't feel a thing.'

Subject: THE HOLY MAN

A Holy man was having a conversation with the Lord one day and said, Lord, I would like to know what Heaven and Hell are like

The Lord led the holy man to two doors

He opened one of the doors and the holy man looked in.

In the middle of the room was a large round table.

In the middle of the table was a large pot of stew which smelled delicious and made the holy man's mouth water

The people sitting around the table were thin and sickly.

They appeared to be famished. They were holding spoons with very long handles that were strapped to their arms and each found it possible to reach into the pot of stew and take a spoonful. But because the handle was longer than their arms, they could not get the spoons back into their mouths.

The holy man shuddered at the sight of their misery and suffering.

The Lord said, 'You have seen Hell. They went to the next room and opened the door. It was exactly the same as the first one

There was the large round table with the large pot of stew which made the holy man's mouth water

The people were equipped with the same long-handled spoons, but here the people were well nourished and plump, laughing and talking.

The holy man said, 'I don't understand.

'It is simple,' said the Lord. 'It requires but one skill...

You see, they have learned to feed each other.

The greedy think only of themselves.'

~~~~~~

An Irishman applying for a job as a blacksmith was asked if he has any experience shoeing[5] horses.
He said no, but he had once told a donkey to piss off.

You were born an original. Don't die a copy.

Don't worry about the world coming to an end today. It is already tomorrow in Australia. ~Charles Schulz

24

Subject: A Drover walks into a bar with a pet crocodile by his side.

He puts the crocodile up on the bar and turns to the astonished patrons. 'I'll do you a deal. I'll open this crocodile's mouth and place my manhood inside.

Then the croc will close his mouth for one minute.

'Then he'll open his mouth and I'll remove my unit unscathed.

In return for witnessing this spectacle, each of you will buy me a drink.'

The crowd murmured their approval.

The man stood up on the bar, dropped his trousers, and placed his credentials and related parts in the crocodile's open mouth.

The croc closed his mouth as the crowd gasped.

After a minute, the man grabbed a beer bottle and smacked the crocodile really, really hard on the top of its head.

The croc opened his mouth and the man removed his genitals unscathed as promised.

The crowd cheered, and the first of his free drinks were delivered.

The man stood up again and made another offer. 'I'll pay anyone $100 who's willing to give it a try.'

A hush fell over the crowd. After a while, a hand went up. A blonde woman timidly spoke up..........

'I'll try it - Just don't hit me so hard with the beer bottle!'

Subject: FEMALE COMPASSION

A man was sitting on a blanket at the beach. He had no arms and no legs.

Three women were walking past and felt sorry for the poor man.

The first woman said 'Have you ever had a hug?'

The man said 'No,' so she gave him a hug and walked on.

The second woman said, 'Have you ever had a kiss?'

The man said, 'No,' so she gave him a kiss and walked on.

The third woman came to him and said, 'Have you ever been fu**ed?'

The fellow's eyes lit up and with a big grin he said, 'No.'

She said, 'You will be when the tide comes in.'

There are two kinds of people,

Those who do the work and those who take the credit.

Try to be in the first group; there is less competition there.

(Indira Gandhi)

The first novel ever written on a typewriter - **Tom Sawyer.**

Subject: THEY WALK AMONGST US EVERY DAY

1) I was checking out at the local Wal-Mart with just a few items and the lady behind me put her things on the belt close to mine. I picked up one of those 'dividers' that they keep by the cash register and placed it between our things so they wouldn't get mixed.

After the girl had scanned all of my items, she picked up the 'divider,' looking it all over for the bar code so she could scan it. Not finding the bar code, she said to me, 'Do you know how much this is?'

I said to her 'I've changed my mind; I don't think I'll buy that today.'

She said 'OK,' and I paid her for the things and left.

She had no clue to what had just happened.

2) A woman at work was seen putting a credit card into her floppy drive and pulling it out very quickly.

When I inquired as to what she was doing, she said she was shopping on the Internet and they kept asking for a credit card number, so she was using the ATM 'thingy'

(keep shuddering!!)

3) I recently saw a distraught young lady weeping beside her car. 'Do you need some help?' I asked.

She replied, 'I knew I should have replaced the battery to this remote door unlocker. Now I can't get into my car. Do you think they (pointing to a distant convenience store) would have a battery to fit this?'

'Hmmm, I don't know. Do you have an alarm, too?' I asked.

'No, just this remote thingy,' she answered, handing it and the car keys to me. As I took the key and manually unlocked the door, I replied, 'Why don't you drive over there and check about the batteries. It's a long walk....'

PLEASE just lay down before you hurt yourself!!!

4) Several years ago, we had an Intern who was none too swift. One day she was typing and turned to a secretary and said, 'I'm almost out of

26

typing paper. What do I do?' 'Just use paper from the photocopier,' the secretary told her. With that, the intern took her last remaining blank piece of paper, put it on the photocopier and proceeded to make five 'blank' copies.

Brunette, by the way!!

5) A mother calls 911 very worried asking the dispatcher if she needs to take her kid to the emergency room, the kid had eaten ants. The dispatcher tells her to give the kid some Benadryl and he should be fine, the mother says, 'I just gave him some ant killer......'
Dispatcher: 'Rush him in to emergency!'
Life is tough. It's even tougher if you're stupid!!!!

Subject: A HELPING HAND
A man and his wife were awakened at 3:00 am by a loud pounding on the door. The man gets up and goes to the door where a drunken stranger, standing in the pouring rain, is asking for a push.
'Not a chance,' says the husband, 'it is 3:00 in the morning!'
He slams the door and returns to bed.
'Who was that?' asked his wife.
'Just some drunk guy asking for a push,' he answers.
'Did you help him?' she asks.
'No, I did not, it is 3:00 in the morning and it is pouring rain out there!'
'Well, you have a short memory,' says his wife. 'Can't you remember about three months ago when we broke down, and those two guys helped us? I think you should help him, and you should be ashamed of yourself!'
The man does as he is told, gets dressed, and goes out into the pounding rain.
He calls out into the dark, 'Hello, are you still there?'
'Yes,' comes back the answer.
'Do you still need a push?' calls out the husband.
'Yes, please!' comes the reply from the dark.
'Where are you?' asks the husband.
'Over here, **on the swing**,' replied the drunk.

When the power of love overcomes the love of power, then the world will know peace. (Jimi Hendrix)

The first product to have a bar code was Wrigley's chewing gum.

Subject: Let's put the seniors in jail, and the criminals in a nursing home.

This way the seniors would have access to showers, hobbies, and walks, they'd receive unlimited free prescriptions, dental and medical treatment, wheel chairs etc. and they'd receive money instead of paying it out.
They would have constant video monitoring, so they could be helped instantly if they fell ...or needed assistance. Bedding would be washed twice a week, and all clothing would be ironed and returned to them. A guard would check on them every 20 minutes, and bring their meals and snacks to their cell. They would have family visits in a suite built for that purpose.
They would have access to a library, weight room, spiritual counselling, pool, and education.
Simple clothing, shoes, slippers, pj's and legal aid would be free, on request. Private, secure rooms for all, and an exercise outdoor yard, with gardens.
Each senior could have a computer (internet access.), TV, radio and daily phone calls.
There would be a board of directors to hear complaints, and the guards would have a code of conduct that would be strictly adhered to.
The "criminals" in a nursing home would get cold food, be left all alone and unsupervised and with lights off at 8pm ...and showers once a week.
They'd live in a tiny room and pay £4,000.00 per month ...and have no hope of ever getting out.

Justice for all

Subject: THE EARRING

A man is at work one day when he notices that his co-worker is wearing an earring. This man knows his co-worker to be a normally conservative fellow, and is curious about his sudden change in 'fashion sense.'
The man walks up to him and says, 'I didn't know you were into earrings.'
'Don't make such a big deal, it's only an earring, 'he replies sheepishly
His friend falls silent for a few minutes, but then his curiosity prods him to say, 'So, how long have you been wearing one?'
'Ever since my wife found it in my car.'

Subject: Advice to an old guy

An old guy (not in the best of shape) was working out in the gym when he spotted a sweet young thing... He asked the trainer that was nearby "What machine in here should I use to impress that sweet thing over there?"
The trainer looked him up and down and said "I would try the ATM in the lobby".......

Subject: BOB

Bob works hard at the office but spends two nights each week bowling, and plays golf every Saturday.

His wife thinks he's pushing himself too hard, so for his birthday she takes him to a local strip club.

The doorman at the club greets them and says, 'Hey, Bob! How ya doin?' His wife is puzzled and asks if he's been to this club before.

'Oh no,' says Bob. 'He's in my bowling league.

When they are seated, a waitress asks Bob if he'd like his usual and brings over a Budweiser.

His wife is becoming increasingly uncomfortable and says, 'How did she know that you drink Budweiser?'

'I recognize her; she's the waitress from the golf club.
I always have a Bud at the end of the 1st nine, honey.'

A stripper then comes over to their table, throws her arms around Bob, starts to rub herself all over him and says, 'Hi Bobby. Want your usual table dance, big boy?'

Bob's wife, now furious, grabs her purse and storms out of the club.

Bob follows and spots her getting into a cab.

Before she can slam the door, he jumps in beside her.

Bob tries desperately to explain how the stripper must have mistaken him for someone else, but his wife is having none of it.

She is screaming at him at the top of her lungs, calling him every 4 letter word in the book...

The cabby turns around and says,
'Geez Bob, you picked up a real bitch this time.'

BOB's hopes to get out of hospital in the next few weeks...

Subject: Golf Balls

A man entered the bus with both of his front pockets full of golf balls and sat down next to a beautiful blonde. The puzzled blonde kept looking at him and his bulging pockets.

Finally, after many such glances from her, he said, "its golf balls."

Nevertheless, the blonde continued to look at him for a very long time, deeply thinking about what he had said.

After several minutes, not being able to contain her curiosity any longer, she asked,

"Does it hurt as much as tennis elbow?"

Subject: WHO DOES WHAT

A man and his wife were having an argument about who should brew the coffee each morning.

The wife said, 'You should do it because you get up first, and then we don't have to wait as long to get our coffee.

The husband said, 'You are in charge of cooking around here and you should do it, because that is your job, and I can just wait for my coffee.'

Wife replies, 'No, you should do it, and besides, it is in the Bible that the man should do the coffee.' Husband replies, 'I can't believe that, show me.'

So she fetched the Bible, and opened the Old Testament and showed him at the top of several pages, that it indeed says. **'HE BREWS'**

Subject: Working for the Council

A bloke goes to the local council to apply for a job in the office.

The interviewer asks him, "Are you allergic to anything?"

He replies, "Yes, caffeine."

"Have you ever worked for the public service before?"

"Yes, I was in the army." he says, "I was in Iraq for two tours."

The interviewer says, "That will give you 5 extra points toward employment."

Then he asks, "Are you disabled in any way?"

The guy says, "Yes. A mine exploded near me when I was there and I lost both of my testicles".

The interviewer grimaces and then says, "O.K. You've got enough points for me to take you on right away. Our normal hours are from 8am to 4pm but you can start tomorrow at 10.00am - and carry on starting at 10.00am every day."

The bloke is puzzled and asks, "If the work hours are from 8.00am to 4.00pm, why don't you want me here until 10.00am? I'm not looking for any special treatment y'know"

"What you have to understand is that this is a council job," the interviewer says,

"For the first two hours, we just stand around drinking coffee and scratching our balls.

There's no point in you coming in for that !!"

A compromise is an agreement whereby both parties get what neither of them wanted.

The cost of raising a medium-size dog to the age of eleven: - £10,120.00

Subject: An Italian Confession

An elderly Italian man who lived on the outskirts of Rimini, Italy, went to the local church for confession.

When the priest slid open the panel in the confessional, the man said:

Bless Me, Father for I have sinned. During World War II, a beautiful Jewish woman from our neighbourhood knocked urgently on my door and asked me to hide her from the Nazis.

So I hid her in my attic."

The priest replied: "That was a wonderful thing you did, and you have no need to confess that."

"There is more to tell, Father. She started to repay me with sexual favours. This happened several times a week, and sometimes twice on Sundays."

The priest said, "That was a long time ago and by doing what you did, you placed the two of you in great danger.

But two people under those circumstances can easily succumb to the weakness of the flesh.

However, if you are truly sorry for your actions, you are indeed forgiven."

"Thank you, Father. That's a great load off my mind. I do have one more question."

"And what is that?" asked the priest.

"Should I tell her the war is over?"

~~~~~~

JUST BEEN GANG RAPED BY A GROUP OF MIME ARTISTS
THEY DID UNSPEAKABLE THINGS TO ME.

~~~~~~

WALT DISNEY WAS AFRAID OF MICE!

~~~~~~

Subject: WORDS

A husband read an article to his wife about how many words women use a day.

30,000 to a man's 15,000.

The wife replied, 'The reason has to be because we have to repeat everything to men.

The husband then turned to his wife and asked, 'What?'

Subject: CREATION

A man said to his wife one day, 'I don't know how you can be so stupid and so beautiful all at the same time.
'The wife responded, 'Allow me to explain.
God made me beautiful so you would be attracted to me;
God made me stupid so I would be attracted to you!

Subject: The Hairdressers

I walked into a hair salon with my husband and three kids in tow and asked loudly,
"How much do you charge for a shampoo and blow job?"
I turned around and walked back out and never went back. My husband didn't say a word...   He knew better.

Subject: Get the door open quickly

Two blondes were in a parking lot trying to unlock the door of their Mercedes with a coat hanger. They tried and tried to get the door open, but they just couldn't! The blonde with the coat hanger stopped for a moment to catch her breath. The other blonde said anxiously, "Hurry up! It's starting to rain and the top is down."

Subject: SHORT ONES

A man inserted an 'ad' in the classifieds: "Wife wanted".
The next day he received five hundred letters. They all said the same thing:
"You can have mine."

Marriage is a relationship in which one person is always right, and the other is a husband.

Two towels in the airing cupboard, which one is in the army
The one on the tank.

If you let go of the past, it no longer has a hold on you.

Subject: QUESTIONS THAT HAUNT ME!

Can you cry under water?

How important does a person have to be before they are considered assassinated instead of just murdered?

Why does a round pizza come in a square box?

What disease did cured ham actually have?

How is it that we put man on the moon before we figured out it would be a good idea to put wheels on luggage?

Why is it that people say they 'slept like a baby' when babies wake up like every two hours?

If a deaf person has to go to court, is it still called a hearing?

Why are you IN a movie, but you're ON TV?

Why do people pay to go up tall buildings and then put money in binoculars to look at things on the ground?

Why do doctors leave the room while you change?
They're going to see you naked anyway...

Why is 'bra' singular and 'panties' plural?

Why do toasters always have a setting that burns the toast to a horrible crisp, which no decent human being would eat?

If the professor on Gilligan's Island can make a radio out of a coconut, why can't he fix a hole in a boat?

If electricity comes from electrons, does morality come from morons?

Why does Goofy stand erect while Pluto remains on all fours? - They're both dogs!

If Wile E. Coyote had enough money to buy all that ACME crap, why didn't he just buy dinner?

If corn oil is made from corn, and vegetable oil is made from vegetables, what is baby oil made from?

Do the Alphabet song and Twinkle, Twinkle Little Star have the same tune? Why did you just try singing the two songs above?

Why do they call it an asteroid when it's outside the hemisphere, but call it a haemorrhoid when it's in your butt?

Did you ever notice that when you blow in a dog's face, he gets mad at you, but when you take him for a car ride, he sticks his head out the window?

Why doesn't Tarzan have a beard?

Subject: Notice in a field:
THE FARMER ALLOWS WALKERS TO CROSS THE FIELD FOR FREE, BUT THE BULL CHARGES.

Subject: Honestly some folk will take offence at anything,
I met a bloke with no legs this morning while at the bus stop'
All I asked was "how are you getting on?"

People want the front of the bus, the back of the church, and the centre of attention.

A patient goes to the doctor and said Help! I've got amnesia what should I do? The doc said "Forget about it!"

Math stuff: 11x11= 121
1111x1111 = 1234321
111111x111111 = 12345654321

Subject: When to start swearing

A 7 year old and a 4 year old are upstairs in their bedroom.

'You know what?' says the 7 year old, 'I think it's about time we started swearing.'

The 4 year old nods his head in approval, so the 7 year old says, 'When we go downstairs for breakfast I'm gonna swear first, then you swear after me, ok?'

'Ok' the 4 year old, agrees with enthusiasm.

The mother walks into the kitchen and asks the 7 year old what he wants for breakfast.

'Oh, shit mum, I don't know, I suppose I'll have some bloody Coco Pops' WHACK!! He flew out of his chair, tumbled across the kitchen floor, got up, and ran upstairs crying his eyes out.

She looked at the 4 year old and asked with a stern voice, ' And what do YOU want for breakfast, young man?'

'I don't know,' he blubbers, 'but it won't be fu*king Coco Pops'

Subject: THE IRISH DAUGHTER

An Irish daughter had not been home for over 5 years. Upon her return, her father cursed her heavily.

'Where have ye been all this time, child? Why did ye not write to us, not even a line? Why didn't ye call? Can ye not understand what ye put yer old mother thru?'

The girl crying, replied, 'sniff, sniff...dad...I became a prostitute.'

'Ye what!? Get out a here, ye shameless harlot! Sinner! You're a disgrace to this Catholic family.'

'OK, Dad... as ye wish. I only came back to give mum this luxurious fur coat, title deed to a ten bedroom mansion, plus a $5 million savings certificate.

For me little brother, this gold Rolex. And for ye daddy, the sparkling new Mercedes Limited Edition convertible that's parked outside plus a membership to the country club,(takes a breath)...and an invitation for ye all to spend New Year's Eve on board my new yacht in the Riviera.'

'What was it ye said ye had become?' says dad.

Girl, crying again, 'A prostitute, daddy! Sniff, sniff.'

'Oh! Be Jesus! Ye scared me half to death, girl! I thought ye said a *protestant*! **Come here and give yer old Dad a big hug!'**

When a clock is hungry, does it go back four seconds.

The King of Hearts is the only king WITHOUT A MOUSTACHE

Subject: What a wife

One day, a man came home and was greeted by his wife dressed in a very sexy nightie. Tie me up, she purred, 'and you can do anything you want.'
So he tied her up and went fishing.

Subject: PADDY

Paddy goes to the vet with his goldfish. "I think it's got epilepsy" he tells the vet.

Vet takes a look and says "It seems calm enough to me".

Paddy says, "I haven't taken it out of the bowl yet".

....

Paddy spies a letter lying on his doormat.

It says on the envelope "DO NOT BEND ".

Paddy spends the next 2 days trying to figure out how to pick the thing up.

....

Paddy shouts frantically into the phone "My wife is pregnant and her contractions are only two minutes apart!"

"Is this her first child?" asks the Doctor.

"No", shouts Paddy, "this is her husband!"

....

Paddy was driving home, drunk as a skunk, suddenly he has to swerve to avoid a tree, then another, then another.

A cop car pulls him over as he veers about all over the road.

Paddy tells the cop about all the trees in the road.

Cop says "For f*** sake Paddy, that's your air freshener swinging about!"

....

Paddy's in jail. Guard looks in his cell and sees him hanging by his feet.

"What are you doing?" he asks. "Hangin' meself" Paddy replies.

"It should be around your neck" says the Guard.

"I tried dat" says Paddy "but I couldn't breathe".

....

An American tourist asks an Irish dive master: "Why do Scuba divers always fall backwards off their boats?"

To which the Irishman replies: "If they fell forwards, they'd still be in the boat."

....

Why are there so many Jones's in the phone book?
Because they all have phones.

....

Subject: Wise words from Father to Daughter

A young woman was about to finish her first year of university. Like so many others her age, she considered herself to be Left Wing Labour Party minded, and she was very much in favour of higher taxes to support her education and for more government programs – in other words, the redistribution of wealth.

She was deeply ashamed that her father was a rather staunch Right Wing blue-ribbon Conservative, a feeling she openly expressed. Based on the lectures that she had attended and the occasional chat with a professor, she felt that her father had for years harboured a selfish desire to keep what he thought should be his.

One day she was challenging her father on his opposition to higher taxes on the rich and the need for more government programs. The self-professed objectivity proclaimed by her professors must be the truth, and she indicated so to her father. He responded by asking how she was doing at university.

Taken aback, she answered rather haughtily that she had a 90% average, and let him know that it was tough to maintain, insisting that she was taking a very difficult course load and was constantly studying, which left her no time to go out and party like other people she knew. She didn't even have time for a boyfriend, and didn't really have many university friends because she spent all her time studying.

Her father listened and then asked, "How is your friend Audrey doing?"

She replied, "Audrey is barely getting by. All she takes are easy classes, she never studies and she barely has a 50% average. She is so popular on campus; university for her is a blast. She's always invited to all the parties, and lots of times she doesn't even show up for classes because she's too hung over."

Her wise father asked his daughter, "Why don't you go to the Dean's office and ask him to deduct 20% off your average and give it to your friend who only has 50%. That way you will both have a 70% average, it would be fair and you would both be equal."

The daughter, visibly shocked by her father's suggestion, angrily fired back, "That's a crazy idea; how would that be fair! I've worked really hard for my grades! I've invested a lot of time, and a lot of hard work! Audrey has done next to nothing toward her degree. She played while I worked my tail off!"

The father slowly smiled, winked and said gently,

"Welcome to the Conservative side of the fence."

Subject: A few short jokes

A mate of mine recently admitted to being addicted to brake fluid. When I quizzed him on it he said not to worry, he could stop any time.

I had a mate who was suicidal. He was really depressed, so I pushed him in front of a train. He was chuffed to bits.

I was at a cash point yesterday when a little old lady asked if I could check her balance, so I pushed her over.

*A new Middle East crisis erupted last night as Dubai Television was refused permission to broadcast 'The Flintstones'. A spokesman for the channel said. "A claim was made that people in Dubai do not understand the humour, but we know for a fact that people in **Abu Dhabi Do.**"*

Subject: One man and his sheep

Man walks into the bedroom with a sheep under his arm while his wife is lying in bed reading.
Man says: 'This is the pig I have sex with when you've got a headache.'
Wife replies: 'I think you'll find that is a sheep.'
Man replies: 'I think you'll find I was talking to the sheep'

....

Subject: Spotted in a safari park:

ELEPHANTS PLEASE STAY IN YOUR CAR.

....

Subject: THE FIGHT

Walking into the bar, Mike said to Charlie the bartender, 'Pour me a stiff one – just had another fight with the little woman.'
'Oh yeah?' said Charlie, 'And how did this one end?'
'When it was over,' Mike replied, 'She came to me on her hands and knees.'
'Really,' said Charles, 'Now that's a switch! What did she say?'
She said, 'Come out from under the bed, you cowardly little chicken.

....

```
        What do you call a fish with no eyes?
                      A fsh.
```

....

It is possible to lead a cow upstairs... but, not downstairs.

....

Subject: AND THE DIFFERENCE IN POLITICAL PARTIES

If a Conservative supporter doesn't like guns, he doesn't buy one.
If a Labour/Green doesn't like guns, they want all guns outlawed.

If a Conservative is a vegetarian, he doesn't eat meat.
If a Labour/Green is a vegetarian, he wants all meat products banned for everyone.

If a Conservative is gay, he quietly leads his life.
If a Labour/Green is gay, he demands legislated respect.

If a Conservative is down-and-out, he thinks about how to better his situation.
A Labour/Green wonders who is going to take care of him.

If a Conservative doesn't like a talk show host, he switches channels.
Labour/Greens demand that those they don't like should be banned.

If a Conservative is a non-believer, he doesn't go to church.
A Labour/Green non-believer wants any mention of God and religion silenced.
(Unless it's a foreign religion, of course!)

If a Conservative reads this, he'll forward it so his friends can have a good laugh.
A Labour/Green will delete it because he's "offended."

Subject: MIRACLE

An Irish priest is driving down to New York and gets stopped for speeding in Connecticut ... The state trooper smells alcohol on the priest's breath and then sees an empty wine bottle on the floor of the car.
He says, 'Sir, have you been drinking?'
'Just water,' says the priest.
The trooper says, 'Then why do I smell wine?'
The priest looks at the bottle and says, 'Good Lord! He's done it again!'

Donkeys kill more people annually than plane crashes or shark attacks. (So, watch your ASS)

Subject: If My Body was a Car - scary how true it is!!

If my body were a car, this is the time I would be thinking about trading it in for a newer model. I've got bumps and dents and scratches in my finish and my paint job is getting a little dull ... But that's not the worst of it.

My headlights are out of focus and it's especially hard to see things up close.

My traction is not as graceful as it once was. I slip and slide and skid and bump into things even in the best of weather.

My whitewalls are stained with varicose veins.

It takes me hours to reach my maximum speed. My fuel rate burns inefficiently.

But here's the worst of it --

Almost every time I sneeze, cough or sputter, either my radiator leaks or my exhaust backfires!

Subject: PENGUIN HEAVEN

Did you ever wonder why there are no dead penguins on the ice in Antarctica –?
Where do they go?
Wonder no more!! !
It is a known fact that the penguin is a very ritualistic bird which lives an extremely ordered and complex life.
The penguin is very committed to its family and will mate for life, as well as maintaining a form of compassionate contact with its offspring throughout its life.
If a penguin is found dead on the ice surface, other members of the family and social circle have been known to dig holes in the ice, using their vestigial wings and beaks, until the hole is deep enough for the dead bird to be rolled into and buried.
The male penguins then gather in a circle around the fresh grave and sing:
"Freeze a jolly good fellow"
"Freeze a jolly good fellow."
Then they kick him in the ice hole.

I have this friend who has a real dilemma. His wife won't give him a divorce until she figures out a way of doing it without making him a happy man.

If you take a laptop computer for a run, will it jog your memory?

What do you call a boomerang that doesn't come back?   *A stick.*

The Wheels of Life

Ed was in trouble. He forgot his wedding anniversary. His wife was really upset. She told him 'Tomorrow morning I expect to find a gift in the driveway that goes from 0 to 200 in under 10seconds AND IT HAD BETTER BE THERE.'
The next morning Ed got up early and left for work. When his wife woke up, she looked out of the window and sure enough there was a small box gift-wrapped in the middle of the driveway.
Confused, she put on her robe, ran out on to the driveway and picked up the box. She opened it and found a brand new bathroom scale.
Funeral services for Ed have been scheduled for Friday.

Subject: Another Blonde Story

A blonde went to the appliance store sale and found a bargain. "I would like to buy this TV," she told the salesman.
"Sorry, we don't sell to blondes," he replied. She hurried home and dyed her hair, then came back and told the salesman "I would like to buy this TV."
"Sorry, we don't sell to blondes," he replied. "Darn, he recognized me," she thought. She went for a complete disguise this time; haircut and new colour, new outfit, big sunglasses, and then waited a few days before she again approached the salesman.
"I would like to buy this TV." "Sorry, we don't sell to blondes," he replied. Frustrated, she exclaimed "How do you know I'm a blonde?"
"Because that's a microwave," he replied.

Subject: Her new Lover

A woman and her friend are visiting the zoo. They are standing in front of the big silver back gorilla's cage when one woman makes a gesture that the gorilla interprets as an invitation. He grabs her, yanks her over the fence, and takes her to his nest in the pen. There he ravishes her and makes passionate love to her for about 2 hours till he is tranquilized, and the lady taken to hospital.

Her friend, deeply concerned, visits her the next day. "Are you hurt?" she asks.

She replies, "Of course I'm hurt! He hasn't called! He hasn't written; no contact at all!!!"

Subject: The Queen and Dolly Parton go to heaven

Queen Elizabeth and Dolly Parton died on the same day and they both go before an Angel to find out if they'll be admitted to Heaven.

Unfortunately, there's only one space left that day.

So the Angel must decide which of them gets in...

The Angel asks Dolly if there's some particular reason why she should go to Heaven.

Dolly takes off her top and says,

'Look at these,

They're the most perfect breasts God ever created,

And I'm sure it will please God to be able to see them every day, for eternity.'

The Angel thanks Dolly, and asks Her Majesty the same question.

The Queen takes a bottle of Perrier out of her purse, drinks it down.

Then, wees into a toilet and pulls the lever.

The Angel Says, 'OK, your Majesty, you may go in.'

Dolly is outraged and asks, 'what was that all about?

I show you two of God's own perfect creations and you turn me down.

She wees into a toilet and she gets in!

Would you explain that to me?'

'Sorry, Dolly,' says the Angel, 'but even in Heaven,

A Royal Flush beats a Pair -   No matter how big they are!

Tried to get tickets to see an Elvis tribute band, but when I phone it keeps saying **press 1 for the money 2 for the show...**

Q. What is the only food that doesn't spoil?

A. Honey

THE 5 BEST SMART ARSED ANSWERS OF THE YEAR

SMART ARSED ANSWER 5
It was mealtime during a flight on a British Airways plane:
"Would you like dinner?" the flight attendant asked the man in the front row.
"What are my choices?" the man asked.
"Yes or no," she replied

SMART ARSED ANSWER 4
A lady was picking through the frozen turkeys at a branch of Sainsbury's[6] store but she couldn't find one big enough for her family.
She asked a passing assistant, "Do these turkeys get any bigger?"
The assistant replied, "I'm afraid not, they're all dead."

SMART ARSED ANSWER 3
The policeman got out of his car and the boy racer he stopped for speeding, rolled down his window.
"I've been waiting for you all day, "the bobby said.
The kid replied, "Well I got here as fast as I could."
When the policeman finally stopped laughing, he sent the kid on his way without a ticket.

SMART ARSED ANSWER 2
A lorry driver was driving along on a country road. A sign came up that read "Low Bridge Ahead."
Before he realised it, the bridge was directly ahead and he got stuck under it.
Cars were backed up for miles. Finally, a police car arrived. The policeman got out of his car and walked to the lorry's cab and said to the driver, "Got stuck, eh?"
The lorry driver said, "No, I was delivering this bridge and ran out of diesel!"

SMART ARSED ANSWER OF THE YEAR
A teacher at a polytechnic college reminded her pupils of tomorrow's final exam.
"Now listen to me, I won't tolerate any excuses for you not being here tomorrow. I might consider a nuclear attack or a serious personal injury, illness, or a death in your immediate family, but that's it, no other excuses whatsoever!"
A smart-arsed chappie at the back of the room raised his hand and asked, "What would happen if I came in tomorrow suffering from complete and utter sexual exhaustion?" The entire class was reduced to laughter and sniggering. When silence was restored, the teacher smiled at the student, shook her head and sweetly said, "Well, I would expect you to write the exam with your other hand."

Subject: In a Nairobi restaurant:
Customers who find our waitresses rude should wait and see the manager.

Subject: THE DOCTOR'S RECEPTIONIST

An older gentleman who had had a prostate operation years before had an appointment to see the urologist in Englewood Florida who shared offices with several other doctors. The waiting room was filled with patients. As he approached the receptionist's desk, he noticed that the receptionist was a large unfriendly woman who looked like a Sumo wrestler. He gave her his name.

In a very loud voice, the receptionist said,

"Yes, I have your name here; you want to see the doctor about impotence, right?"

All the patients in the waiting room snapped their heads around to look at the very embarrassed man. He recovered quickly, and in an equally loud voice replied, 'NO, I'VE COME TO INQUIRE ABOUT A SEX CHANGE OPERATION, BUT I DON'T WANT THE SAME DOCTOR THAT DID YOURS.'

The room erupted in applause!

Subject: GETTING HOME LATE

David staggered home very late after another evening with his drinking buddy, Paddy. He took off his shoes to avoid waking his wife, Kathleen.

He tiptoed as quietly as he could toward the stairs leading to their upstairs bedroom, but misjudged the bottom step. As he caught himself by grabbing the banister, his body swung around and he landed heavily on his rump. A whiskey bottle in each back pocket broke and made the landing especially painful.

Managing not to yell, David sprung up, pulled down his pants, and looked in the hall mirror to see that his butt cheeks were cut and bleeding. He managed to quietly find a full box of Band-Aids and began putting a Band-Aid as best he could on each place he saw blood...

He then hid the now almost empty Band-Aid box and shuffled and stumbled his way to bed.

In the morning, David woke up with searing pain in both his head and butt and Kathleen staring at him crossly

She said, 'You were drunk again last night weren't you?'

David said, 'Why you say such a mean thing?'

'Well,' Kathleen said, 'it could be the open front door, it could be the broken glass at the bottom of the stairs, it could be the drops of blood trailing through the house, it could be your bloodshot eyes, but mostly .... it's all those Band-Aids stuck on the hall mirror.

44

Subject: BLISS

An old man and woman were married for many years even though they hated each other. Whenever there was a confrontation, yelling could be heard deep into the night. The old man would shout, "When I die, I will dig my way up and out of the grave and come back and haunt you for the rest of your life!"

Neighbours feared him. They believed he practiced black magic because of the many strange occurrences that took place in their neighbourhood.

The old man liked the fact that he was feared. To everyone's relief, he died of a heart attack when he was 98. His wife had a closed casket at the wake.

After the burial, she went straight to the local bar and began to party, as if there were no tomorrow.

Her neighbours, concerned for her safety, asked, "Aren't you afraid that he may indeed be able to dig his way out of the grave and haunt you for the rest of your life?"

The wife put down her drink and said,

"Let him dig! I had him buried upside down, and you know men won't ask for directions!!"

Subject: VISIT TO THE DENTIST

The female dentist pulls out a numbing needle to give the man a shot.

"No way! No needles. I hate needles," the patient said.

The dentist starts to hook up the nitrous oxide and the man objects.

"I can't do the gas thing. The thought of having the gas mask on suffocates me!"

The dentist then asks the patient if he has any objection to taking a pill.

"No objection," the patient says. "'I'm fine with pills."

The dentist then returns and says, "Here's a Viagra."

The patient says, "Wow! I didn't know Viagra worked as a pain killer!"

"It doesn't" said the dentist, "but it's going to give you something to hold onto when I pull your tooth.

Fred walked into a psychiatrist's office wearing only cling film. The psychiatrist said:
Well, I can clearly see you're nuts.

Life in the Australian Army...

Text of a letter from a kid from Eromanga to Mum and Dad. (For those of you not in the know, Eromanga is a small town, west of Quilpie in the far south west of Queensland)

Dear Mum & Dad,

I am well. Hope youse are too. Tell me big brothers Doug and Phil that the Army is better than workin' on the station - tell them to get in bloody quick smart before the jobs are all gone! I wuz a bit slow in settling down at first, because ya don't hafta get outta bed until 6am. But I like sleeping in now, cuz all ya gotta do before brekky is make ya bed and shine ya boots and clean ya uniform. No bloody horses to get in, no calves to feed, no troughs to clean - nothin'!! Ya haz gotta shower though, but it's not so bad, coz there's lotsa hot water and even a light to see what ya doing!

At brekky ya get cereal, fruit and eggs but there are no kangaroo steaks or goanna stew like wot Mum makes. You don't get fed again until noon and by that time all the city boys are buggered because we've been on a 'route march' - geez it's only just like walking to the windmill in the bullock paddock!!

This one will kill me brothers Doug and Phil with laughter. I keep getting medals for shootin' - dunno why. The bull's eye is as big as a bloody dingo's arse and it don't move and it's not firing back at ya like the Johnsons did when our big scrubber bull got into their prize cows before the Ekka last year! All ya gotta do is make yourself comfortable and hit the target - it's a piece of piss!! You don't even load your own cartridges, they comes in little boxes, and ya don't have to steady yourself against the roll bar of the roo shooting truck when you reload!

Sometimes ya gotta wrestle with the city boys and I gotta be real careful coz they break easy - it's not like fighting with Doug and Phil and Jack and Boori and Steve and Muzza all at once like we do at home after the muster. Turns out I'm not a bad boxer either and it looks like I'm the best the platoon's got, and I've only been beaten by this one bloke from the Engineers - he's 6 foot 5 and 15 stone and three pick handles across the shoulders and as ya know I'm only 5 foot 7 and eight stone wringin' wet, but I fought him till the other blokes carried me off to the boozer.

I can't complain about the Army - tell the boys to get in quick before word gets around how bloody good it is.

Your loving daughter,
Susan.

Subject: Lovemaking Tips For Seniors

1. Wear your glasses to make sure your partner is actually in the bed.
2. Set timer for 3 minutes, in case you doze off in the middle.
3. Set the mood with lighting. (Turn them ALL OFF!)
4. Make sure you put 911 on your speed dial before you begin...
5. Write partner's name on your hand in case you can't remember.
6. Use extra polygrip so your teeth don't end up under the bed.
7. Have Tylenol ready in case you actually complete the act...
8. Make all the noise you want....the neighbours are deaf, too.
9. If it works, call everyone you know with the good news!!
10. Don't even think about trying it twice.

'OLD' IS WHEN...
Your sweetie says, 'Let's go upstairs and make love,' and you answer, 'Pick one; I can't do both!'
'OLD' IS WHEN...
Your friends compliment you on your new alligator shoes and you're barefoot.
'OLD' IS WHEN...
Going bra-less pulls all the wrinkles out of your face.
'OLD' IS WHEN....
You don't care where your spouse goes, just as long as you don't have to go along.
'OLD' IS WHEN.....
You are cautioned to slow down by the doctor instead of by the police.
'OLD' IS WHEN...
'Getting a little action' means you don't need to take a laxative today.
'OLD' IS WHEN.....
'Getting lucky' means you find your car in the parking lot.....
'OLD' IS WHEN...
An 'all nighter' means not getting up to use the bathroom.
'OLD' IS WHEN....
You're not sure if these are facts or jokes.

They reckon that Beer contains female hormones and I think they are right. After 8 pints I talk shit and can't drive!

Future aircraft will be piloted by a man and a dog. The man is there to feed the dog, and the dog is there to keep the man from touching the controls

Subject: Wee Scottish Tale.

A golfer is cupping his hand to scoop water from a Highland burn on the St Andrews course.

A groundskeeper shouts: 'Dinnae drink tha waater! Et's foo ae coo's shite an pish![7]

The golfer replies: 'My Good fellow, I'm from England. Could you repeat that for me, in English, please!?'

The keeper replies: 'I said, use both hands – you'll spill less that way!'

Subject: *Lee Trevino - a true story*

One day, shortly after joining the PGA tour in 1965, Lee Trevino, a professional golfer and married man, was at his home in Dallas, Texas mowing his front lawn, as he always did.

A lady driving by in a big, shiny Cadillac stopped in front of his house, lowered the window and asked,

"Excuse me, do you speak English?"

Lee responded, "Yes M'aam, I do"

The lady then asked, "What do you charge to do yard work?"

Lee said, "Well, the lady in this house lets me sleep with her".

The lady hurriedly put the car into gear and sped off.

Subject: FIRST OF THE OLYMPIC JOKES

It's 2012 and it's the Olympics in London.

A Scotsman, an Englishman and an Irishman want to get in, but they haven't got tickets.

The Scotsman picks up a manhole cover, tucks it under his arm and walks to the gate.

"McTavish, Scotland," he says, "Discus" and in he walks.

The Englishman picks up a length of scaffolding and slings it over his shoulder.

"Waddington-Smith, England "he says, "Pole vault" and in he walks.

The Irishman looks around and picks up a roll of barbed wire and tucks it under his arm.

"O'Malley, Ireland "he says, "Fencing."

After all, what is your host's purpose in having a party? Surely not for you to enjoy yourself. If that were their sole purpose, they'd have simply sent champagne and women over to your place by taxi. ~ P.J. O'Rourke

Subject: MORE SHORT JOKES

Vicar booking into a hotel asks the receptionist "Is the Porn channel in my room disabled" "No" she replies "it's just regular porn you sick bastard"

A mate of mine has just told me he's shagging his girlfriend and her twin, I said how can you tell them apart, he said "Her brothers got a moustache!"

A biker goes to the Doctor with hearing problems "Can you describe the symptoms to me"
"Yes.....Homer is a fat yellow lazy bastard and Marge is a skinny bird with big blue hair.

Wife gets naked & asks hubby,
'What turns you on more, my pretty face or my sexy body?'Hubby looks her up & down and replies 'Your sense of humour!'

Subject: DEATH NOTICE

When the husband finally died his wife put the usual death notice in the paper, but added that he died of gonorrhoea.
No sooner were the papers delivered when a friend of the family phoned and complained bitterly, 'You know very well that he died of diarrhoea, not gonorrhoea.' Replied the widow, 'I nursed him night and day so of course I know he died of diarrhoea, but I thought it would be better for posterity to remember him as a great lover rather than the big fat shit he always was.'

Grandma's Birth Control Pills

A doctor that had been seeing an 80-year-old woman for most of her life finally retired.
At her next check-up, the new doctor asked her to bring all the medicines that had been prescribed for her. As the young doctor was looking through the medicines, his eyes grew wide as he realized she had a prescription for birth control pills.
"Mrs. Smith, do you realize these are BIRTH CONTROL PILLS?"
"Yes, they help me sleep at night."
"Mrs. Smith, I assure you there is absolutely NOTHING in these that could possibly help you sleep at night."
She reached out and patted the young doctor's knee.
"Yes dear, I know that. But every morning I grind one up and mix it in the glass of orange juice that my 16 year old granddaughter drinks. And believe me; it helps me sleep EVERY night.

Alcohol does make you more attractive to the opposite sex.
After they've drunk enough of it.

Subject: **Notes left in milk bottles**

Dear milkman:
I've just had a baby, please leave another one.

Please leave an extra pint of paralysed milk.

Cancel one pint after the day after today.

Please don't leave any more milk. All they do is drink it.

Milkman, please close the gate behind you because the birds keep pecking the tops off the milk.

Milkman, please could I have a loaf but no bread today.

Please cancel milk. I have nothing coming into the house but two sons on the dole.

Sorry not to have paid your bill, but my wife had a baby and I've been carrying it around in my pocket for weeks.

Sorry about yesterday's note. I didn't mean one egg and a dozen pints, but the other way round.

When you leave my milk please knock on my bedroom window and wake me because I want you to give me a hand to turn the mattress.

Please knock. My TV's broken down and I missed last night's Coronation Street[8]. If you saw it, will you tell me what happened over a cup of tea?

My daughter says she wants a milkshake. Do you do it before you deliver or do I have to shake the bottle?

Please send me a form for cheap milk, for I have a baby two months old and did not know about it until a neighbour told me.

Please send me details about cheap milk as I am stagnant.

Milk is needed for the baby. Father is unable to supply it.

From now on please leave two pints every other day and one pint on the days in between, except Wednesdays and Saturdays when I don't want any milk.

My back door is open. Please put milk in 'fridge, get money out of cup in drawer and leave change on kitchen table in pence, because we want to play bingo tonight.

Please leave no milk today. When I say today, I mean tomorrow, for I wrote this note yesterday.

No milk. Please do not leave milk at No. 14 either as he is dead until further notice.

Subject: An elderly couple were on a cruise and it was really stormy.

They were standing on the back of the boat watching the moon, when a wave came up and washed the old woman overboard. They searched for days and couldn't find her, so the captain sent the old man back to shore with the promise that he would notify him as soon as they found something. Three weeks went by and finally the old man got a fax from the boat. It read: 'Sir, sorry to inform you, we found your wife dead at the bottom of the ocean. We hauled her up to the deck and attached to her butt was an oyster and in it was a pearl worth $50,000. Please advise.' The old man faxed back:

'Send me the pearl and re-bait the trap.'

Subject: SECOND TIME AROUND

A funeral service is being held for a woman who has just passed away. At the end of the service, the pall bearers are carrying the casket out when they accidentally bump into a wall, jarring the casket. They hear a faint moan. They open the casket and find that the woman is actually alive! She lives for ten more years, and then dies. Once again, a ceremony is held, and at the end of it, the pall bearers are again carrying out the casket. As they carry the casket towards the door, the husband cries out,

'Watch that wall!'

Hedgehogs - why can't they just share the hedge?

Subject: MABEL & ETHEL

Two elderly women were eating breakfast in a restaurant one morning. Ethel noticed something funny about Mabel's ear and she said, "Mabel, do you know you've got a suppository in your left ear?' Mabel answered, 'I have a suppository in my ear?' She pulled it out and stared at it. Then she said, 'Ethel, I'm glad you saw this thing. Now I think I know where to find my hearing aid.'

Subject: THE OLD LADY

When I went to lunch today, I noticed an old lady sitting on a park bench sobbing her eyes out. I stopped and asked her what was wrong.
She said, 'I have a 22 year old husband at home. He makes love to me every morning and then gets up and makes me pancakes, sausage, fresh fruit and freshly ground coffee.'
I said, 'Well, then why are you crying?'
She said, 'He makes me homemade soup for lunch and my favourite brownies and then makes love to me for half the afternoon.
I said, 'Well, why are you crying?'
She said, 'For dinner he makes me a gourmet meal with wine and my favourite dessert and then makes love to me until 2:00 a.m. '
I said, 'Well, why in the world would you be crying?'
She said, 'I can't remember where I live!'

Subject: SENIORS SUPERSEX

A little old lady who had lost her marbles was running up and down the halls in a nursing home.
As she walked, she would flip up the hem of her nightgown and say "Supersex."
She walked up to an elderly man in a wheelchair, flipping her gown at him, she said, "Supersex."
He sat silently for a moment or two and finally answered, "I'll take the soup."

In a City restaurant:

OPEN SEVEN DAYS A WEEK, AND WEEKENDS TOO.

If you ever need a helping hand, there is one at each end of your arms.

He who feels that he is too small, to make a difference, has never been bitten by a mosquito.

Subject: THE HUNTING TRIP

Two Irishmen flew to Canada on a hunting trip. They chartered a small plane to take them into the Rockies for a week hunting moose.
They managed to bag 6. As they were loading the plane to return, the Pilot said the plane could take only 4 moose.
The two lads objected strongly. "Last year we shot six. The pilot let us take them all and he had the same plane as yours."
Reluctantly, the pilot gave in and all six were loaded. The plane took off.
However, while attempting to cross some mountains even on full power the little plane couldn't handle the load and went down.
Somehow, surrounded by the moose bodies, only Paddy and Mick survived the crash.
After climbing out of the wreckage, Paddy asked Mick, "Any idea where we are?"
Mick replied, "I think we're pretty close to where we crashed last year."

Subject: NUN

A man suffered a serious heart attack while shopping in a store. The store staff called 999 when they saw him collapse to the floor. The paramedics rushed the man to the nearest hospital where he had emergency open heart bypass surgery.
He awoke from the surgery to find himself in the care of nuns at the Catholic Hospital he was taken to. A nun was seated next to his bed holding a clip board loaded with several forms, and a pen. She asked him how he was going to pay for his treatment.
"Do you have health insurance?" she asked.
He replied in a raspy voice, "No health insurance."
The nun asked, "Do you have money in the bank?"
He replied, "No money in the bank."
"Do you have a relative who could help you with the payments?" asked the irritated nun.
He said, "I only have a Spinster sister, and she is a nun."
The nun became agitated and announced loudly, "Nuns are not spinsters! Nuns are married to God."
The patient replied, "Perfect. Send the bill to my brother-in-law."

Subject: Secrets to a long and happy marriage

An old woman was sipping a glass of wine, while sitting on the patio with her husband, and she says "I love you so much. I don't know how I could ever live without you"
Her husband asks "Is that you or the wine talking?"
She replies "It's me ... talking to the WINE

Subject: IDIOT SIGHTING 1

My daughter and I went through the McDonalds take-away window and I gave the girl a £5 note. Our total was £4.20, so I also handed her a 20 pence piece.
She said, 'you gave me too much money.'
I said, 'Yes I know, but this way you can just give me £1 back.'
She sighed and went to get the manager who asked me to repeat my request. I did so, and he handed me back the 20 pence and said 'We're sorry but they could not do that kind of thing here.'
The girl then proceeded to give me back 80 pence in change.
Do not confuse the girls at MacD's.

IDIOT SIGHTING 2

We had to have the garage door repaired. The GARADOR repairman told us that one of our problems was that we did not have a 'large' enough motor on the opener.
I thought for a minute, and said that we had the largest one GARADOR made at that time, a ½ horsepower. He shook his head and said, 'Lady, you need a ¼ horsepower.' I responded that ½ was larger than ¼ and he said, 'NOOO, it's not. Four is larger than two.'
We haven't used Garador repair since. Happened in Bromley, Kent UK

IDIOT SIGHTING 3

I live in a semi rural area. We recently had a new neighbour call the Highways Department to request the removal of the DEER CROSSING sign on our road. The reason:
'Too many deer are being hit by cars out here! I don't think this is a good place for them to be crossing anymore.'
Story from Crayford, Kent, UK

IDIOT SIGHTING 4

My daughter went to a local Kentucky Fried and ordered a Mexican taco. She asked the person behind the counter for 'minimum lettuce.' He said he was sorry, but they only had iceberg lettuce.
From Gillingham Kent, UK.

IDIOT SIGHTING 5

I was at the airport, checking in at the gate when an Irish airport employee asked, 'Has anyone put anything in your baggage without your knowledge?'
To which I replied, 'If it was without my knowledge, how would I know?'
He smiled knowingly and nodded, 'That's why we ask.'
Happened Heathrow Airport .... UK

IDIOT SIGHTING 6

The stoplight on the corner buzzes when it's safe to cross the street. I was crossing with an intellectually challenged co-worker of mine. She asked if I knew what the buzzer was for. I explained that it signals blind people when the light is red. Appalled, she responded, 'What on earth are blind people doing driving?!'
She is a Local County Council employee in Dartford Kent, UK

IDIOT SIGHTING 7

When my husband and I arrived at our local Ford dealer to pick up our car; we were told the keys had been locked in it. We went to the service department and found a mechanic working feverishly to unlock the driver's side door. As I watched from the passenger side, I instinctively tried the door handle and discovered that it was unlocked. 'Hey,' I announced to the Mechanic " It's open!' His reply, 'I know. I already did that side.'
This was at the Ford dealership in St Albans, Hertfordshire UK .

Subject: DOWN AT THE RETIREMENT CENTRE
80-year old Bessie bursts into the recreation room at the retirement home. She holds her clenched fist in the air and announces, "Anyone who can guess what's in my hand can have sex with me tonight!!"
An elderly gentleman in the rear shouts out, "An elephant?"
Bessie thinks a minute and says, "Close enough."

I was watching the London Marathon and saw one runner dressed as a chicken and another runner dressed as an egg.
 I thought: 'This could be interesting'

Subject: *THE BANKER*

A Banker parks his brand new Porsche in front of the office to show it off to his colleagues.
As he's getting out of the car, a lorry comes speeding along too close to the kerb and takes off the door before zooming off.
More than a little distraught, the Banker grabs his mobile and calls the police.
Five minutes later, the police arrive. Before the policeman has a chance to ask any questions, the man starts screaming hysterically: "My Porsche, my beautiful silver Porsche is ruined. No matter how long it's at the panel beaters, it'll simply never be the same again!'
After the man finally finishes his rant, the policeman shakes his head in disgust.
"I can't believe how materialistic you bloody Bankers are," he says. "You lot are so focused on your possessions that you don't notice anything else in your life."
"How can you say such a thing at a time like this?" sobs the Porsche owner.
The policeman replies, "Didn't you realise that your right arm was torn off when the truck hit you?"
The Banker looks down in horror.
"F***ING HELL!" he screams.........."Where's my Rolex ????"

Subject: Getting a hairdryer through customs...

A distinguished young woman on a flight from Ireland asked the Priest beside her, 'Father, may I ask a favour?' 'Of course, child. What may I do for you?'
'Well, I bought an expensive woman's electronic hair dryer for my mother's birthday that is unopened and well over the Customs' limits, and I'm afraid they'll confiscate it. Is there any way you could carry it through Customs for me? Under your robes perhaps?'
'I would love to help you, dear, but I must warn you: I will not lie.'
'With your honest face, Father, no one will question you. 'When they got to Customs, she let the priest go ahead of her.
The official stopped the Father and asked, 'Father, do you have anything to declare?'
'From the top of my head down to my waist, I have nothing to declare.'
The official thought this answer strange, so asked, 'And what do you have to declare from your waist to the floor?'
'I have a marvellous instrument designed to be used on a woman, but which is, to date, unused.'
Roaring with laughter, the official said, 'Go ahead, Father. Next!'

Subject: ROMANCE

An older couple were lying in bed one night. The husband was falling asleep but the wife was in a romantic mood and wanted to talk.
She said: "You used to hold my hand when we were courting.."
Wearily he reached across, held her hand for a second and tried to get back to sleep.
A few moments later she said: "Then you used to kiss me."
Mildly irritated, he reached across, gave her a peck on the cheek and settled down to sleep.
Thirty seconds later she said: "Then you used to bite my neck.."
Angrily, he threw back the bed clothes and got out of bed.
"Where are you going?" she asked..
"To get my teeth!"

Subject: SENIOR DRIVING 1

As a senior citizen was driving down the motorway, his car phone rang.
Answering, he heard his wife's voice urgently warning him, "Vernon, I just heard on the news that there's a car going the wrong way on the M25. Please be careful!"
"Crikey"said Vernon , "It's not just one car.. It's hundreds of them!"

SENIOR DRIVING 2

Two elderly women were out driving in a large car - both could barely see over the dashboard. As they were cruising along, they came to major crossroad. The stop light was red, but they just went on through.
The woman in the passenger seat thought to herself "I must be losing it. I could have sworn we just went through a red light." After a few more minutes, they came to another major junction and the light was red again. Again, they went right through. The woman in the passenger seat was almost sure that the light had been red but was really concerned that she was losing it. She was getting nervous.
At the next junction, sure enough, the light was red and they went on through. So, she turned to the other woman and said, "Mildred, did you know that we just ran through three red lights in a row? You could have killed us both!"
Mildred turned to her and said, "Oh! Am I driving?"

My mother never saw the irony in calling me a son-of-a-bitch.

The bank sent a cheque back marked "Insufficient funds".
Them or me?

Subject: OLD FRIENDS

Two elderly ladies had been friends for many decades. Over the years, they had shared all kinds of activities and adventures. Lately, their activities had been limited to meeting a few times a week to play cards. One day, they were playing cards when one looked at the other and said, "Now don't get mad at me. I know we've been friends for a long time but I just can't think of your name. I've thought and thought, but I can't remember it. Please tell me what your name is."

Her friend glared at her. For at least three minutes she just stared and glared at her. Finally she said, "How soon do you need to know?"

Subject: Dog Missing

An old Irish farmer's dog goes missing and he's inconsolable.

His wife says "Why don't you put an advert in the paper?"

He does, but two weeks later the dog is still missing

"What did you put in the paper?" his wife asks.

"Here boy" he replies.

Subject: The Blonde and the Farmer

A blonde decided that she was tired of her empty life. She cut her hair and dyed it brown, and set off for a drive.

She wanted to do random acts of kindness to see if it would change her life.

While driving through the countryside, she came across a farmer who was trying to get his sheep across the road. She stopped her car and waved the farmer across, thinking this would be her first good deed. After the sheep had all crossed, the blonde said to the farmer,

"Your sheep are so cute. If I guess how many there are, could I have one." The farmer thought it impossible and told the blonde it was okay.   "237", said the blonde.

The farmer was amazed that the blonde had guessed the exact number, but lived up to his bargain.

"I'll take that feisty one over there", said the blonde.

Then the farmer said to the blonde, "Okay, now if I guess the real colour of your hair, can I have my dog back?

THE INLAND REVENUE v PADDY

The Inland Revenue decides to audit Paddy, and summons him to an appointment with the most thorough auditor in the office. The auditor is not surprised when Paddy shows up with his solicitor.

The auditor says, "Well, sir, you have an extravagant lifestyle and no full-time employment, which you explain by saying that you win money gambling. I'm not sure the Inland Revenue finds that believable."

"I'm a great gambler, and I can prove it," says Paddy. "How about a demonstration?"

The auditor thinks for a moment and says, "Okay. You're on!"

Paddy says, "I'll bet you a thousand pound that I can bite my own eye."

The auditor thinks a moment and says, "No way! It's a bet."

Paddy removes his glass eye and bites it. The auditor's jaw drops.

Paddy says, "Now, I'll bet you two thousand pound that I can bite my other eye."

The auditor can tell Paddy isn't blind, so he takes the bet.

Paddy removes his dentures and bites his good eye.

The stunned auditor now realises he has bet and lost three thousand quid, with Paddy's solicitor as a witness. He starts to get nervous.

"Would you like to go double or nothing?" Paddy asks. "I'll bet you six thousand pound that I can stand on one side of your desk and pee into that rubbish bin on the other side, and never get a drop anywhere in between."

The auditor, twice burned, is cautious now, but he looks carefully and decides there's no way Paddy can manage that stunt, so he agrees again.

Paddy stands beside the desk and unzips his trousers, but although he strains like hell, he can't make the stream reach the bin on other side, so he pretty much urinates all over the auditor's desk.

The auditor leaps with joy, realising that he has just turned a major loss into a big win. But Paddy's solicitor moans and puts his head in his hands.

"Are you okay?" the auditor asks.

"Not really," says the solicitor. "This morning, when Paddy told me he'd been summoned for an audit, he bet me £20,000 that he could come in here and p*ss all over your desk - and that you'd be happy about it!"

Never throw away a clock. It's a waste of time

99 percent of lawyers give the rest a bad name

Subject: Why Some Men Have Dogs And Not Wives:

1. The later you are, the more excited your dogs are to see you.

2. Dogs don't notice if you call them by another dog's name.

3. Dogs don't mind if you leave a lot of things on the floor.

4. A dog's parents never visit.

5. Dogs agree that you have to raise your voice to get your point across.

6. You never have to wait for a dog; they're ready to go 24 hours a day.

7. Dogs find you amusing when you're drunk.

8. Dogs like to go hunting and fishing.

9. A dog will not wake you up at night to ask, "If I died, would you get another dog?"

10. If a dog has babies, you can put an ad in the paper and give them away.

11. A dog will let you put a studded collar on it without calling you a pervert.

12. If a dog smells another dog on you, they don't get mad. They just think it's interesting.

13. Dogs like to ride in the back of a pickup truck.

14. If a dog leaves, it won't take half of your stuff.

Subject: George

I was out with one of my best drinking buddies, George, and he was talking about marriage, and then his wife. He drank some, then said, "Well, what it comes down to it... well... my wife knows nothing of my wants and needs... she's hardly ever in the mood for sex... I guess what it comes down to is that my wife just doesn't understand me at all, does yours?"

I thought about it a minute or two, then said. "I don't think so George, as a matter of fact; I don't recall her ever even mentioning your name at all."

I went to buy some camouflage trousers the other day but I couldn't find any.

THE LARGER THE LAKE OF KNOWLEDGE THE LONGER THE SHORE OF WONDER

History Mystery

Abraham Lincoln was elected to Congress in 1846.
John F. Kennedy was elected to Congress in 1946.

Abraham Lincoln was elected President in 1860.
John F. Kennedy was elected President in 1960.

Both were particularly concerned with civil rights.
Both wives lost their children while living in the White House.

Both Presidents were shot on a Friday.
Both Presidents were shot in the head

Now it gets really weird.

Lincoln 's secretary was named Kennedy.
Kennedy's Secretary was named Lincoln .

Both were assassinated by Southerners.
Both were succeeded by Southerners named Johnson.

Andrew Johnson, who succeeded Lincoln , was born in 1808.
Lyndon Johnson, who succeeded Kennedy, was born in 1908.

John Wilkes Booth, who assassinated Lincoln , was born in 1839.

Lee Harvey Oswald, who assassinated Kennedy, was born in 1939.

Both assassins were known by their three names.
Both names are composed of fifteen letters.

Now hang on to your seat.

Lincoln was shot at the theatre named 'Ford'.
Kennedy was shot in a car called 'Lincoln' made by 'Ford'.

Lincoln was shot in a theatre and his assassin ran and hid in a warehouse.
Kennedy was shot from a warehouse and his assassin ran and hid in a theatre.

Booth and Oswald were assassinated before their trials.

Subject: Thomas Cook Holidays - listing some of the guests' complaints during the season

1. "I think it should be explained in the brochure that the local store does not sell proper biscuits like custard creams or ginger nuts."
2. "It's lazy of the local shopkeepers to close in the afternoons. I often needed to buy things during 'siesta' time - this should be banned
3. "On my holiday to Goa in India, I was disgusted to find that almost every restaurant served curry. I don't like spicy food at all."
4. "We booked an excursion to a water park but no-one told us we had to bring our swimming costumes and towels."
5. A tourist at a top African game lodge overlooking a water hole, who spotted a visibly aroused elephant, complained that the sight of this rampant beast ruined his honeymoon by making him feel "inadequate".
6. A woman threatened to call police after claiming that she'd been locked in by staff. When in fact, she had mistaken the "do not disturb" sign on the back of the door as a warning to remain in the room.
7. "The beach was too sandy."
8. "We found the sand was not like the sand in the brochure. Your brochure shows the sand as yellow but it was white."
9. A guest at a Novotel in Australia complained his soup was too thick and strong. He was inadvertently slurping the gravy at the time.
10. "Topless sunbathing on the beach should be banned. The holiday was ruined as my husband spent all day looking at other women."
11. "We bought' Ray-Ban' sunglasses for five Euros (£3.50) from street trader, only to find out they were fake."
12. "No-one told us there would be fish in the sea. The children were startled."
13. "There was no egg slicer in the apartment..."
14. "We went on holiday to Spain and had a problem with the taxi drivers as they were all Spanish..."
15. "The roads were uneven."
16. "It took us nine hours to fly home from Jamaica to England. It only took the Americans three hours to get home."
17. "I compared the size of our one-bedroom apartment to our friends' three-bedroom apartment and ours was significantly smaller."
18. "The brochure stated: 'No hairdressers at the accommodation'. We're trainee hairdressers - will we be OK staying here?"
19. "There are too many Spanish people.. The receptionist speaks Spanish. The food is Spanish. Too many foreigners."
20. "We had to queue outside with no air conditioning."
21.. "It is your duty to advise us of noisy guests before we travel."
22. "I was bitten by a mosquito - no-one said they could bite."

They walk amongst us and they Vote and BREED!!!

Subject: Politically Correctness
A London bobby spots a huge black guy dancing on the roof of a Ford Sierra car.
He radios for backup.
"Give me a sit rep?"
"A big fat darkie is dancing on a car roof."
You can't say that over the radio" replies the operator,
"You have to use the politically correct terminology"
"OK" he says,
"Zulu ....Tango ....Sierra"

Subject: WOULD YOU PASS THIS TEST
You are driving down the road in your sports car on a wild, stormy night, when you pass by a bus stop and you see three people waiting for the bus:

1. An old lady who looks as if she is about to die
2. A very old friend who once saved your life.
3. The perfect partner you have been dreaming about.

Which one would you choose to offer a ride to, knowing that there could only be one passenger in your car?
Think before you continue reading.
This is a moral/ethical dilemma that was once actually used as part of a job application.
You could pick up the old lady, because she is going to die, and thus you should save her first.
Or you could take the old friend because he once saved your life, and this would be the perfect chance to pay him back.
However, you may never be able to find your perfect mate again
The candidate who was hired (out of 200 applicants) had no trouble coming up with his answer. He simply answered:
I would give the car keys to my old friend and let him take the lady to the hospital.
I would stay behind and wait for the bus with the partner of my dreams.
Sometimes, we gain more if we are able to give up our stubborn thought limitations.
Never forget to 'Think Outside of the Box.'

HOWEVER......
The correct answer is to run the old lady over and put her out of her misery, have sex with the perfect partner on the bonnet of the car, then drive off with the old friend for a few beers.

Subject: WHAT I OWE MY MOTHER:

1. My mother taught me TO APPRECIATE A JOB WELL DONE.
'If you're going to kill each other, do it outside. I just finished cleaning.'

2. My mother taught me RELIGION.
'You better pray that this will come out of the carpet.'

3. My mother taught me about TIME TRAVEL
'If you don't straighten up, I'm going to knock you into the middle of next week!'

4. My mother taught me LOGIC .
' Because I said so, that's why.'

5.My mother taught me MORE LOGIC .
'If you fall out of that swing and break your neck, you're not going out.'

6. My mother taught me FORESIGHT.
'Make sure you wear clean underwear, in case you're in an accident.'

7. My mother taught me IRONY.
'Keep crying, and I'll give you something to cry about.'

8. My mother taught me about the science of OSMOSIS.
'Shut your mouth and eat your supper.'

9. My mother taught me about CONTORTIONISM .
'Will you look at that dirt on the back of your neck!'

10. My mother taught me about STAMINA
'You'll sit there until all that SOUP is gone.'

11. My mother taught me about WEATHER .
'This room of yours looks as if a tornado went through it.'

12. My mother taught me about HYPOCRISY
'If I told you once, I've told you a million times. Don't exaggerate!'

13. My mother taught me the CIRCLE OF LIFE .
'I brought you into this world, and I can take you out.'

14. My mother taught me about BEHAVIOUR MODIFICATION.
'Stop acting like your father!'

15. My mother taught me about ENVY.
'There are millions of less fortunate children in this world who don't have wonderful parents like you do. '

16. My mother taught me about ANTICIPATION.
'Just wait until we get home.'

17. My mother taught me about RECEIVING .
'You are going to get it when you get home!'

18. My mother taught me MEDICAL SCIENCE.
'If you don't stop crossing your eyes, they are going to get stuck that way.'

19. My mother taught me ESP .
'Put your sweater on; don't you think I know when you are cold?'

20. My mother taught me HUMOUR .
'When that lawn mower cuts off your toes, don't come running to me..'

21. **My mother taught me HOW TO BECOME AN ADULT** .
'If you don't eat your vegetables, you'll never grow up.'
22. **My mother taught me GENETICS**.
'You're just like your father.'
23. **My mother taught me about my ROOTS**.
'Shut that door behind you. Do you think you were born in a field?'
24. **My mother taught me WISDOM**.
'When you get to be my age, you'll understand.'
25. And my favourite:
My mother taught me about JUSTICE
'One day you'll have kids, and I hope they turn out just like you '

Subject: How to tell if your wife or your dog loves you more

You put your wife and the dog in the boot[9] of your car; go inside and watch a full 2 hour movie on TV.

After 2 hours you return to the car and open the boot.

Which one is pleased to see you?

If I knew grandchildren were going to be this much fun, I would have had them first!

Subject: HYMN 365

A minister was completing a temperance sermon. With great emphasis he said, 'If I had all the beer in the world, I'd take it and pour it into the river.' With even greater emphasis he said, 'And if I had all the wine in the world, I'd take it and pour it into the river.'

And then finally, shaking his fist in the air, he said, 'And if I had all the whiskey in the world, I'd take it and pour it into the river.'

Sermon complete, he sat down.

The song leader stood very cautiously and announced with a smile, nearly laughing, 'For our closing song, let us sing Hymn 365,

'Shall We Gather at the River.'

A little girl was diligently pounding away on her grandfather's computer.

"What are you doing" he asked.

She told him she was writing a story.

"What's it about?" he asked.

"I don't know," she replied. "I can't read."

Subject :FW: LADY OF THE NIGHT

There was a guy sitting at a bar having a beer. Up walks a so called "lady of the night". She says,
"For $300, I'll do anything you want."
Our fine lad thinks for a moment then says:
Ok. Paint my house!

Subject: Fwd: FW: Thinking On Your Feet

A man in London walked into the produce section of his local Tesco's[10] supermarket and asked to buy half a head of lettuce. The boy working in that department told him that they only sold whole heads of lettuce. The man was insistent that the boy ask the manager about the matter. Walking into the back room, he boy said to the manager, "Some old bastard wants to buy a half a head of lettuce."
As he finished his sentence, he turned around to find that the man was standing right behind him, so he quickly added,
"and this gentleman kindly offered to buy the other half."
The manager approved the deal and the man went on his way.
Later, the manager said to the boy,"
I was impressed with the way you got yourself out of that situation earlier, we like people who can think on their feet here, and where are you from son?"
" New Zealand , sir," the boy replied.
"Why did you leave New Zealand ?" the manager asked.
The boy said, "Sir, there's nothing but prostitutes and rugby players there."
"Is that right?" replied the manager," My wife is from New Zealand !"
"Really?" replied the boy,
"Who'd she play for?"

God may have created man before woman, but there is always a rough draft before the masterpiece

How is it one careless match can start a forest fire, but it takes a whole box to start a campfire?

Some people say "If you can't beat them, join them". I say "If you can't beat them, beat them", because they will be expecting you to join them, so you will have the element of surprise.

Subject: Fwd: To make you smile!

The Irish have solved their own fuel problems. They imported 50 billion tonnes of sand from the Arabs and they're going to drill for their own oil.

My mate's missus left him last Thursday; she said she was going out for a pint of milk & never come back!
I asked him how he was coping and he said, "Not bad, I've been using that powdered stuff."

The police came to my front door last night holding a picture of my wife.
They said, "Is this your wife, sir?"
Shocked, I answered, " Yes."
They said, "I'm afraid it looks like she's been hit by a bus."
I said, "I know, but she has a lovely personality."

Two Irishmen are hammering floorboards down in a house.
Paddy picks up a nail, realises it's upside down & throws it away.
He carries on doing this until Murphy says, "Why are you throwing them away?"
"Because they're upside down," says Paddy.
"You daft prat," replies Murphy, "save 'em for the ceiling!!"

A Professor of Mathematics sent a fax to his wife which read

"Dear wife, you must realise that you are 54 years old and I have certain needs which you are no longer able to satisfy. I am otherwise happy with you as a wife and I sincerely hope you will not be hurt or offended to learn that by the time you read this letter I will be at the Grand Hotel with my 18 year old teaching assistant. I'll be home before midnight"
When he arrived at the hotel there was a fax waiting for him that read
"Dear husband, you too are 54 and by the time you read this I will be at the Park Hotel with the 18 year old pool boy. Being the brilliant mathematician that you are, you can easily appreciate the fact that 18 goes into 54 a lot more times than 54 goes into 18. Don't wait up".

Two Irishmen find a mirror in the road.
The first one picks it up & says, "Blow me I know this face but I can't put a name to it."
The second picks it up & says, "You daft bastard it's me!"

Subject: Little Johnny joke.

A grade three teacher is giving a lesson on nutrition, and she decides to ask her students what they had for breakfast.

To add a spelling component, she asks the students to also spell their answers.

Susan puts up her hand and says she had an egg, 'E-G-G'.

'Very good', says the teacher.

Peter says he had toast 'T-O-A-S-T'.   'Excellent.'

Johnny has his hand up and the teacher reluctantly calls on him.

I had bugger all', he says, ' B-U-G-G-E-R-A-L-L'.

The teacher is mortified and scolds Johnny for his rude answer.

Later when the lesson turns to geography, she asks the students some rudimentary questions.

Susan correctly identifies the Capital of Canada. Peter is able to tell her which ocean is off Canada 's east coast.

When it's Johnny's turn, the teacher remembers his rude answer from the nutrition lesson, and decides to give him a very difficult question.

Johnny, she asks, 'Where is the Pakistani border?'

Johnny ponders the question and finally says, 'The Pakistani boarder is in bed with my mother.

That's why I got bugger all for breakfast'.

A couple drove down a country road for several miles, not saying a word. An earlier discussion had led to an argument and neither of them wanted to concede their position..

As they passed a barnyard of mules, goats, and pigs, the husband asked sarcastically, 'Relatives of yours?'   'Yep,' the wife replied, 'in-laws.'

Subject: I've often been asked, 'What do you old folks do now that you're retired?

Well, I'm fortunate to have a chemical engineering background. One of the things I enjoy most is turning beer, wine, Scotch , and margaritas into urine.

Life is good, live it.

I've just had a letter back from **Screwfix**. they said they regretted to inform me that they're not actually a dating agency.

Subject: The Towel

Some years ago, in a small coastal Irish community, Paddy married a woman, Maggie, who was half his age. All was well at first until Maggie took delivery of a "woman's magazine" and began to read things about sex. It soon became clear that she had never climaxed during sex and, according to her Grandmother, all Irish women are entitled to a climax once in a while.

To resolve the problem, Paddy and Maggie went to see the Veterinarian, since there was no doctor within thirty miles who could be relied upon not to gossip.

However, the Vet didn't have a clue, but he did recall how, during hot summers, his mother and father would fan a cow with a big towel, that was having difficulty breeding. Apparently, this cooled her down and helped her to relax. So he recommended they hire a strong, virile young man to wave a big towel over them while they were having sex. This, the Vet said, should cause the young wife to cool down, relax and possibly achieve the sought after climax.

So the couple hired a strong young man from Dublin to wave a huge bath towel over them as the Vet suggested.

After many efforts, Maggie still had not climaxed so they went back to the Vet who suggested she change partners and let the young man have a go while Paddy waved the big towel.

They tried it that night and Maggie went into wild, screaming, ear-splitting climaxes, one right after the other for about two and a half hours.

When it was over, Paddy looked down at the exhausted young man and in a boasting voice shouted,

"And that, me auld son, is how ya wave a feckin' towel!"

Subject: <u>UNDERSTANDING WOMEN</u>

(A MAN'S PERSPECTIVE)

I know I'm not going to understand women.

I'll never understand how you can take boiling hot wax, pour it onto your upper thigh, rip the hair out by the root, and still be afraid of a spider.

The first couple to be shown in bed together on prime time TV was Fred and Wilma Flintstone

Subject: FW: Grandma Still Drives – PRICELESS

Grandma is eighty-eight years old and still drives her own car. She writes:

Dear Grand-daughter,

The other day I went up to our local Christian book store and saw a 'Honk if you love Jesus bumper sticker' I was feeling particularly sassy that day because I had just come from a thrilling choir performance, followed by a thunderous prayer meeting. So, I bought the sticker and put it on my bumper. Boy, am I glad I did; what an uplifting experience that followed.

I was stopped at a red light at a busy intersection, just lost in thought about the Lord and how good he is, and I didn't notice that the light had changed. It is a good thing someone else loves Jesus because if he hadn't honked, I'd never have noticed. I found that lots of people love Jesus!

While I was sitting there, the guy behind started honking like crazy, and then he leaned out of his window and screamed, 'For the love of God!'

'Go! Go! Go! Jesus Christ, GO!'

What an exuberant cheerleader he was for Jesus!

Everyone started honking! I just leaned out my window and started waving and smiling at all those loving people. I even honked my horn a few times to share in the love!

There must have been a man from Florida back there because I heard him yelling something about a sunny beach.

I saw another guy waving in a funny way with only his middle finger stuck up in the air.

I asked my young teenage grandson in the back seat what that meant.

He said it was probably a Hawaiian good luck sign or something.

Well, I have never met anyone from Hawaii, so I leaned out the window and gave him the good luck sign right back. My grandson burst out laughing. Even he was enjoying this religious experience!!

A couple of the people were so caught up in the joy of the moment that they got out of their cars and started walking towards me. I bet they wanted to pray or ask what church I attended, but this is when I noticed the light had changed. So, grinning, I waved at all my brothers and sisters, and drove on through the intersection.

I noticed that I was the only car that got through the intersection before the light changed again and felt kind of sad that I had to leave them after all the love we had shared. So I slowed the car down, leaned out the window and gave them all the Hawaiian good luck sign one last time as I drove away. Praise the Lord for such wonderful folks!!

Will write again soon,

Love, Grandma

Subject: Bob and the Blonde

Bob, a handsome dude, walked into a sports bar around 9:58 pm. He sat down next to a blonde at the bar and stared up at the TV.

The 10 pm news was coming on. The news crew was covering the story of a man on the ledge of a large building preparing to jump.

The blonde looked at Bob and said, "Do you think he'll jump?"

Bob said, "You know, I bet he'll jump." The blonde replied, "Well, I bet he won't."

Bob placed a $20 bill on the bar and said, "You're on!"

Just as the blonde placed her money on the bar, the guy on the ledge did a swan dive off the building, falling to his death.

The blonde was very upset, but willingly handed her $20 to Bob, saying, "Fair's fair. Here's your money."

Bob replied, "I can't take your money. I saw this earlier on the 5 pm news, and so I knew he would jump."

The blonde replied, "I did too, but didn't think he'd do it again."

Bob took the money...

Subject: Stuck in the countryside

Seems that the travelling salesman was driving in the country and his car broke down. He hiked several miles to a farm house, and asked the farmer if there was a place he could stay overnight.

"Sure," said the farmer, "my wife died several years ago, and my 2 daughters are 21 and 23 but they're off to college, and I'm all by myself, so I have lots of room to put you up."

Hearing this, the salesman turned around and started walking back towards the highway, and the farmer called after him. "Didn't you hear what I said? I have lots of room."

"I heard you," said the salesman, "but I think I'm in the wrong joke."

Subject: AT THE CHECKOUT

As she was unloading her items on the conveyor belt to check out, a drunk standing behind her watched as she placed the items in front of the cashier.

While the cashier was ringing up her purchases, the drunk calmly stated, 'You must be single.' The woman was a bit startled by this proclamation, but she was intrigued by the derelict's intuition, since she was indeed single. She looked at her six items on the belt and saw nothing particularly unusual about her selection that could have tipped off the drunk to her marital status. Curiosity getting the better of her, she said, 'Well, you know what, you're absolutely correct. But how on earth did you know that?'

The drunk replied, 'Cos you're ugly.'

Subject: NUMBERS

The teacher asked little Johnny if he knows his numbers.
"Yes," he said. "I do. My father taught me."
"Good. What comes after three?" "Four," answers the boy.
"What comes after six?" "Seven."
"Very good," says the teacher. "Your dad did a good job. What comes after ten?"
"A Jack."

Subject: COWS

Is it just me, or does anyone else find it amazing that during the Foot & Mouth scare that the government could track a single cow, born in the back of North Yorkshire almost three years ago, right to the stall where she slept in Lincolnshire ? And, they even tracked her calves to their stalls. But they are unable to locate 1,000,000 illegal immigrants wandering around our country.
Maybe we should give each of them a cow.

Subject: 'Circumcised'

A teacher noticed that a little boy at the back of the class was squirming around, scratching his crotch, and not paying attention.
She went back to find out what was going on.
He was quite embarrassed and whispered that he had just recently been circumcised and he was quite itchy.
The teacher told him to go down to the principal's office.
He was told to telephone his mother and ask her what he should do about it. He did and returned to his class.
Suddenly, there was a commotion at the back of the room.
She went back to investigate only to find him sitting at his desk with his 'private part' hanging out.
'I thought I told you to call your mum!' she said.
'I did,' he said, 'And she told me that if I could stick it out until lunchtime, she'd come and pick me up from school.

I've just heard the window cleaner shouting and swearing outside my house. I think he's lost his rag.

Subject: FW: : Brian

A man walked out to the street and caught a taxi just going by. He got into the taxi, and the cabbie said, "Perfect timing. You're just like "Brian!

Passenger: "Who?"

Cabbie: "Brian Sullivan. He's a guy who did everything right all the time. Like my coming along when you needed a cab, things happen like that to Brian Sullivan, every single time."

Passenger: "There are always a few clouds over everybody."

Cabbie: "Not Brian Sullivan. He was a terrific athlete. He could have won the Grand Slam at tennis. He could golf with the pros. He sang like an opera baritone and danced like a Broadway star and you should have heard him play the piano. He was an amazing guy."

Passenger: "Sounds like he was something really special."

Cabbie: "There's more. He had a memory like a computer. He remembered everybody's birthday. He knew all about wine, which foods to order and which fork to eat them with. He could fix anything. Not like me. I change a fuse, and the whole street blacks out. But Brian Sullivan, he could do everything right."

Passenger: "Wow. Some guy then."

Cabbie: "He always knew the quickest way to go in traffic and avoid traffic jams. Not like me, I always seem to get stuck in them. But Brian, he never made a mistake, and he really knew how to treat a woman and make her feel good. He would never answer her back even if she was in the wrong; and his clothing was always immaculate, shoes highly polished too. He was the perfect man! He never made a mistake. No one could ever measure up to Brian Sullivan."

Passenger: "An amazing fellow. How did you meet him?"

Cabbie: "Well, I never actually met Brian.

He died. I'm married to his f**ing widow."**

Subject: Inner Peace

If you can start the day without caffeine,
If you can always be cheerful, ignoring aches and pains,
If you can resist complaining and boring people with your troubles,
If you can eat plain food every day and be grateful for it,
If you can understand when your loved ones are too busy to give you any time,
If you can take criticism and blame without resentment,
If you can conquer tension without medical help,
If you can relax without liquor,
If you can sleep without the aid of drugs,...
Then You Are Probably ....
The Family Dog!

Police raided Kermit's lily pad and found 100s of nude pictures of Miss Piggy. They said it was the worst case of frogs' porn ever seen.

Subject: *DO YOU WANT TO GO TO HEAVEN*

Father Murphy walks into a pub in Donegal, and asks the first man he meets, 'Do you want to go to heaven?' The man said, 'I do, Father...'
The priest said, 'Then stand over there against the wall.'
Then the priest asked the second man, 'Do you want to go to heaven?'
'Certainly, Father,' the man replied.
'Then stand over there against the wall,' said the priest.
Then Father Murphy walked up to O'Toole and asked, 'Do you want to go to heaven?'
O'Toole said, 'No, I don't Father.'
The priest said, 'I don't believe this. You mean to tell me that when you die you don't want to go to heaven?'
O'Toole said, 'Oh, when I die, yes. I thought you were getting a group together to go right now.'

Ultimate chat-up line:
Does this handkerchief smell of chloroform?"

Subject: INTERESTING FACTS:

"Stewardesses"   Is the longest word typed with only the left hand
==

And "lollipop"   Is the longest word typed only with your right hand.
==

No word in the English language rhymes with month, orange, silver, or purple.
==

"Dreamt" is the only English word that ends in the letters "mt".
==

Our eyes are always the same size from birth,
But our nose and ears never stop growing.
==

The sentence: "The quick brown fox jumps over the lazy dog" uses every letter of the alphabet.
==

The words 'racecar', 'kayak', 'level, 'deed', 'level', 'pip', 'rotor', 'civic', 'pop', 'madam,' 'eye', 'nun', 'radar', 'toot', (there are many more.) are the same whether they are read left to right or right to left (palindromes) ('redivider' is the longest in common usage)
==

There are only four words in the English language which end in "dous": tremendous, horrendous, stupendous, and hazardous
==

There are two words in the English language that have all five vowels in order: "abstemious" and "facetious."
==

TYPEWRITER is the longest word that can be made using the letters only on one row of the keyboard.
==

A cat has 32 muscles in each ear.
==

A goldfish has a memory span of three seconds.
==

A "jiffy" is an actual unit of time for 1/100th of a second.
==

A shark is the only fish that can blink with both eyes.
==

A snail can hibernate for three years.
==

===
Almonds are a member of the peach family.
===

An ostrich's eye is bigger than its brain.
(I know some people like that also)
===

Babies are born without kneecaps
===

February 1865 is the only month in recorded history not to have a full moon.
===

In the last 4,000 years, no new animals have been domesticated.
===

If the population of China walked past you, 8 abreast, the line would never end because of the rate of reproduction.
===

Leonardo Da Vinci invented the scissors.
===

Peanuts are one of the ingredients of dynamite!
===

Rubber bands last longer when refrigerated.
===

The average person's left hand does 56% of the typing.
===

The cruise liner, QE 2 moves six inches for each gallon of diesel it burns.
===

The microwave was invented after a researcher walked by a radar tube and a chocolate bar melted in his pocket.   (Good thing he did that.)
===

The winter of 1932 was so cold that Niagara Falls froze completely solid.
===

There are more chickens than people in the world.
===

Winston Churchill was born in a ladies' room during a dance.
===

Women blink nearly twice as much as men.
===

Bonus!! All the ants in Africa weigh more than ALL the Elephants!!
===

In a Calcutta Coffee House:
People discarding cigarette stubs in cups will be served coffee in ash trays.

Subject: When girls don't come on!!

This was written by a guy!!!

I never quite figured out why the sexual urge of men and women differ so much. And I never have figured out the whole Venus and Mars thing. I have never figured out why men think with their head and women with their heart.

FOR EXAMPLE:

One evening last week, my girlfriend and I were getting into bed. Well, the passion starts to heat up, and she eventually says, 'I don't feel like it, I just want you to hold me.'

I said, 'WHAT??!! What was that?!'

So she says the words that every boyfriend on the planet dreads to hear...

'You're just not in touch with my emotional needs as a woman enough for me to satisfy your physical needs as a man.'

She responded to my puzzled look by saying, 'Can't you just love me for who I am and not what I do for you in the bedroom?'

Realizing that nothing was going to happen that night, I went to sleep.

The very next day I opted to take the day off of work to spend time with her. We went out to a nice lunch and then went shopping at a big, big department store. I walked around with her while she tried on several different very expensive outfits. She couldn't decide which one to take, so I told her we'd just buy them all. She wanted new shoes to compliment her new clothes, so I said, 'Let's get a pair for each outfit.'

We went on to the jewellery department where she picked out a pair of diamond earrings. Let me tell you. She was so excited. She must have thought I was one wave short of a shipwreck. I started to think she was testing me because she asked for a tennis bracelet when she doesn't even play tennis.

I think I threw her for a loop when I said, 'That's fine, honey.' She was almost nearing sexual satisfaction from all of the excitement. Smiling with excited anticipation, she finally said, 'I think this is all dear, let's go to the cashier.'

I could hardly contain myself and I blurted out, 'No honey, I don't feel like it.' Her face just went completely blank as her jaw dropped with a baffled, 'WHAT?'

I then said, 'Honey! I just want you to HOLD this stuff for a while. You're just not in touch with my financial needs as a man enough for me to satisfy your shopping needs as a woman.'

And just when she had this look like she was going to kill me, I added, 'Why can't you just love me for who I am and not for the things I buy you?'

Apparently I'm not having sex tonight either... but at least the bitch knows I'm smarter than she thought.

Subject: IRISH STORIES

An Irishman who had a little too much to drink is driving home from the city one night and, of course, his car is weaving violently all over the road. A cop pulls him over. "So," says the cop to the driver, 'where have ya been?" "Why, I've been to the pub of course," slurs the drunk.
"Well," says the cop, "it looks like you've had too much to drink this evening."
"I did all right," the drunk says with a smile.
"Did you know," says the cop, standing straight and folding his arms across his chest, "that a few intersections back, your wife fell out of your car?" Oh, thank heavens," sighs the drunk. "For a minute there, I thought I'd gone deaf."

==

Brenda O'Malley is home making dinner, as usual, when Tim Finnegan arrives at her door
"Brenda, may I come in?" he asks. "I've somethin' to tell ya".
"Of course you can come in, you're always welcome, Tim. But where's my husband?"
"That's what I'm here to be telling ya, Brenda. There was an an accident down at the Guinness brewery."
"Oh, God no!" cries Brenda. "Please don't tell me."
"I must, Brenda. Your husband Shamus is dead and gone. I'm sorry."
Finally, she looked up at Tim. "How did it happen, Tim?"
"It was terrible, Brenda. He fell into a vat of Guinness Stout and drowned."
"Oh my dear Jesus! But tell me true, Tim. Did he at least go quickly?"
Well, Brenda…..no. In fact, he got out three times to have a pee."

==

Mary Clancy goes up to Father O'Grady after his Sunday morning service and she's in tears.
He says, "So what's bothering you, Mary my dear?"
She says, "Oh, Father, I've got terrible news. My husband died last night."
The priest says, "Oh, Mary, that's terrible. Tell me, Mary, did he have any last requests?"
She says. "That he did, Father."
The priest says, "What did he ask, Mary?"
She says, "He said, 'Please, Mary, put down that damn gun. '"

==

A drunk staggers into a Catholic Church, enters a confessional booth, sits down but says nothing. The Priest coughs a few times to get his attention but the drunk continues to sit there. Finally, the Priest pounds three times on the wall.
The drunk mumbles, "Ain't no use knocking, there's no paper on this side either."

Subject: *The Girl Lodger*

A Scottish couple took in an 18-year-old girl as a lodger. She asked if she could have a bath, but the woman of the house told her they didn't have a bath, although if she wanted to, she could use a tin bath in front of the fire.

"Monday's the best night, when my husband goes out to darts," she said. The girl agreed to have a bath the following Monday.

After her husband had gone to the pub for his darts match, the woman filled the bath and watched the girl get undressed. She was surprised to see that the lass didn't have any pubic hair. She mentioned this to her husband when he came home. He didn't believe her, so she said:

"Next Monday, when you go to darts, leave a little early and wait in the back garden. I'll leave a gap in the curtains so you can see for yourself."

So the following Monday, while the girl again got undressed, the wife asked: "Do you shave?"   "No," replied the girl. "I've just never grown any hair down there. Do you have hair?"

"Oh, yes," said the woman, and she pulled up her nightdress and showed the girl that she was really generously endowed in the hair department.....very generously indeed.

The girl finished her bath and went to bed.

Later that night, when the husband came in, the wife asked him, "Did you see it?"

"Yes," he said, "but why the hell did you have to show her yours."

"Why ever are you worried about that?" she said. "You've seen it often enough before."

"I know," he said, "but the darts team hadn't!"

Subject: GREAT JOB

A man went to Harley Street, London and saw a card advertising for a Gynaecologist's Assistant. Interested, he went in and asked the clerk for details.

The clerk pulled out the file and read:

The job entails getting the ladies ready for the gynaecologist.

You have to help the women out of their underwear, lay them down and carefully wash their private regions, then apply shaving foam and gently shave off their pubic hair, then rub in soothing oils so they're ready for the gynaecologist's examination.

The annual salary is £65,000, and if you're interested you'll have to go to Manchester .

"My God, is that where the job is?" asked the man.

"No sir" she answered, "that's where the end of the queue is."

Subject: Lost In Translation

I will never hear or see this word again without thinking of this joke.

Today's word is................ **Fluctuations**

I was at my bank today; there was a short line.

There was just one lady in front of me, an Asian lady who was trying to exchange yen for dollars.

It was obvious she was a little irritated.

She asked the teller, "Why it change? Yesterday, I get two hunat dolla fo yen. Today I only get hunat eighty? Why it change?"

The teller shrugged his shoulders and said, "Fluctuations."

The Asian lady says, "Fluc you white people too"

Smart little lady

Little Emily went home from school and told her mum that the boys kept asking her to do cartwheels because she's very good at them.

Mum said, "You should say "No" -they only want to look at your knickers."

Emily said, "I know they do.

That's why I hide them in my schoolbag"!

Subject: Drink Driving

I would just like to share an experience with you and it has to do with drinking and driving. As you know I have had brushes with the authorities on the way home from the odd event over the years. Well I have done something about it:

Last night I was out for a few drinks with some friends and had way too much beer and wine. Knowing full well I was drunk; I did something I've never done before. I took a bus home. I arrived home safely and without incident which was a real surprise, since I had never driven a bus before!

Subject: *Seen during a London conference:*

For anyone who has children and doesn't know it, there is a day care centre on the 1st floor.

I just had a call from a charity asking me to donate some of my clothes to the starving people throughout the world.

I told them to bugger off.

Anybody who fits into my clothes isn't starving.

Subject: *I think we all need a laugh* !!!!!

I dialled a number and got the following recording:** **
"I am not available right now, but thank you for caring enough to call.
I am making some changes in my life.
Please leave a message after the beep. If I do not return your call,
You are one of the changes."
****

A small Boy wrote to Santa Claus," send me a brother."
Santa wrote back, "SEND ME YOUR MOTHER."
****

What is the definition of Mistress?
Someone between the Mister and Mattress.
****

What's the difference between stress, tension and panic?*
Stress is when wife is pregnant,*
Tension is when girlfriend is pregnant,*
and Panic is when both are pregnant.*
****

A young boy asks his Dad, "What is the difference between confident and
confidential?"*
Dad says, "You are my son, I'm confident about that.
Your friend, over there, is also my son, that's confidential."
****

A three-year-old boy was examining his testicles while taking a bath.
Mom" he asked, "are these my brains?"
"Not yet," she replied.
****

Subject: ONCE UPON A TIME

Once upon a time, a guy asked a girl... 'Will you marry me?'
The girl said, 'NO!'
And the guy lived happily ever after and rode motorcycles and
went fishing and hunting and played golf and sailed a lot and
drank beer and scotch and had tons of money in the bank and left
the toilet seat up and discarded his clothes on the bedroom floor
and farted whenever he wanted.
The end

We live in a society where pizza gets to your house before the police.

Subject: The Difference Between Grandfathers and Grandmothers

A friend, who worked away from home all week, always made a special effort with his family on the weekends. Every Sunday morning he would take his 7-year old granddaughter out for a drive in the car for some bonding time -- just him and his granddaughter. One particular Sunday however, he had a bad cold and really didn't feel like being up at all. Luckily, his wife came to the rescue and said that she would take their granddaughter out.

When they returned, the little girl anxiously ran upstairs to see her Grandfather. 'Well, did you enjoy your ride with grandma?'

'Oh yes, Granddad' the girl replied, 'and do you know what? We didn't see a single arsehole, blind bastard, dip shit or wanker anywhere we went today!'

Subject: Never Trust A Sailor

A pretty, young blonde woman in Liverpool was so depressed that she decided to end her life by throwing herself into the ocean.

She went down to the docks and was about to leap into the frigid water when a handsome young sailor saw her tottering on the edge of the pier, crying.

He took pity on her and said, "Look, you have so much to live for. We're off to Hawaii in the morning. If you like, I can stow you away on my ship.. I'll take good care of you and bring you food every day. "Moving closer, he slipped his arm around her waist and added, "I'll keep you happy, and you'll keep me happy."

The blonde nodded. What did she have to lose? Perhaps a fresh start in Hawaii would give her life new meaning.

That night, the sailor took her aboard and hid her in the bowels of the ship. From then on, he brought her three sandwiches and a piece of fruit every night, and they made passionate love until dawn.

Two weeks later, she was discovered by the Captain during a routine inspection. "What are you doing here?" he asked.

"I have an arrangement with one of the sailors," she explained. "I get food and a trip to Hawaii , and in return he's screwing me."

"He certainly is," said the Captain. "This is the Liverpool Ferry."

I started so many fights at my school –
I had that attention-deficit disorder. So I didn't finish a lot of them.

What do the Irish call a cocktail?
A pint of Guinness with a potato in it.

Subject: Funny Chinese

Got a Chinese last night. On way home in the car I heard the bag rustle. I looked over to see a pair of eyes looking out of the top of the bag at me then disappear back inside. I was so scared I nearly crashed the car. I looked again, saw the eyes looking at me then disappear again, I went straight back to the shop with the bag terrified. I asked the Chinese guy, "what is going on"?

He said "u no worry, it Peking duck".!!!!!!!!!!!!!!!!

Subject: Fwd: FW: Airlines desk attendant

An award should go to the Virgin Airlines desk attendant in Sydney some months ago for being smart and funny, while making her point, when confronted with a passenger who probably deserved to fly as cargo.

A crowded Virgin flight was cancelled after Virgin's 767s had been withdrawn from service. A single attendant was re-booking a long line of inconvenienced travellers. Suddenly an angry passenger pushed his way to the desk. He slapped his ticket down on the counter and said, "I HAVE to be on this flight and it HAS to be FIRST CLASS".

The attendant replied, "I'm sorry, sir. I'll be happy to try to help you, but I've got to help these people first. I'm sure we'll be able to work something out "
The passenger was unimpressed. He asked loudly, so that the passengers behind him could hear, "DO YOU HAVE ANY IDEA WHO I AM?"

Without hesitating, the attendant smiled and grabbed her public address microphone: "May I have your attention, please, may I have your attention please," she began - her voice heard clearly throughout the terminal.

"We have a passenger here at Desk 14 WHO DOES NOT KNOW WHO HE IS. If anyone can help him find his identity, please come to Desk 14."

With the folks behind him in line laughing hysterically, the man glared at the Virgin attendant, gritted his teeth and said,"F*** You!"

Without flinching, she smiled and said,
"I'm sorry, sir, but you'll have to get in line for that too."

Subject: Is Murphy dead or alive?

Two tough union men were working on a building site when Murphy fell from the second floor scaffolding. "Are ya dead?" cried Gallagher from above. "To be sure I am," replied Murphy. "You are such a liar Murphy that I don't know whether to believe you or not!" called Gallagher. "That proves I'm dead," said Murphy's voice from the rubble below, because if I was alive, you wouldn't be game to call me a liar!!

Subject: One afternoon at Cheers, Cliff Clavin was explaining the Buffalo Theory to his buddy Norm. Here's how it went

"Well ya see, Norm, it's like this.... A herd of buffalo can only move as fast as the slowest buffalo. And when the herd is hunted, it is the slowest and weakest ones at the back that are killed first This natural selection is good for the herd as a whole, because the general speed and health of the whole group keeps improving by the regular killing of the weakest members.

In much the same way, the human brain can only operate as fast as the slowest brain cells. Excessive intake of alcohol, as we know, kills brain cells. But naturally, it attacks the slowest and weakest brain cells first. In this way, regular consumption of beer eliminates the weaker brain cells, making the brain a faster and more efficient machine. That's why you always feel smarter after a few beers."

Subject: A doctor was addressing a large audience in Oxford...

"The material we put into our stomachs should have killed most of us sitting here, years ago.

Red meat is full of steroids and dye. Soft drinks corrode your stomach lining. Chinese food is loaded with MSG. High transfat diets can be fatal and none of us realizes the long-term harm caused by the germs in our drinking water. But, there is one thing that is the most dangerous of all and most of us have, or will eat it. Can anyone here tell me what food it is that causes the most grief and suffering for years after eating it?"

After several seconds of quiet, a 70-year-old man in the front row raised his hand, and softly said,

"Wedding Cake."

Subject: It's Murphy again!!!

Murphy dropped dead the moment he arrived home from a vacation in the tropics. He was laid out in the coffin for friends and neighbours to pay their last respects. "He's got a great tan," Mrs Doolan from next door mused. "The holiday did him the world of good." "And he looks so calm and serene," said Mrs McGuiness. "That's because he died in his sleep." explained Mrs Murphy, "and he doesn't know he's dead yet, but when he wakes up, the shock will kill him!"

Subject: Bottle of Merlot

A man asked a waiter to take a bottle of Merlot to an unusually attractive woman sitting alone at a table in a cosy little restaurant.

So the waiter took the Merlot to the woman and said, 'This is from the gentleman who is seated over there.'.... and indicated the sender with a nod of his head.

She stared at the wine coolly for a few seconds, not looking at the man, then, decided to send a reply to him by a note.

The waiter, who was lingering nearby for a response, took the note from her and conveyed it to the gentleman.

The note read: 'For me to accept this bottle, you need to have a Merc in your garage, a million dollars in the bank and 7 inches in your pants'.

After reading the note, the man decided to compose one of his own.

He folded the note, handed it to the waiter and instructed him to deliver it to the lady.

It read:

'Just to let you know things aren't always what they appear to be. I have a Ferrari Maranello, BMW Z8, Mercedes CL600, and a Porsche Turbo in my several garages; I have beautiful homes in Aspen and Miami , and a 10,000 acre ranch in Louisiana . There is over twenty million dollars in my bank account and portfolio. But, not even for a woman as beautiful as you, would I cut off three inches. Just send the wine back.

Subject: Molly

A society lady runs into the employment office one day and demands a maid "right now". It seems she's having a dinner party that night and her maid quit. The guy in the agency explains that all the girls he has right now have just gotten off the boat from Ireland. They're untrained. The lady says she'll train the girl but needs someone right away. The agency guy asks for volunteers and Molly comes forward. She agrees to go and be trained. Well, the dinner party comes and goes and works out just fine. Molly does a great job. The next morning, the lady's walking along the upstairs hall and sees Molly in one of the guest rooms. Looks like she's making the bed but she's just standing there. Curious, the woman walks in and looks over Molly's shoulder. There on the bed lies a condom. The lady turns bright red and tries to laugh it off.

"Why Molly," she says, "Surely you have those in Ireland, don't you?"

Molly: "Sure we do madam, but we don't skin em."

85

Subject: Tale of the Irish Sausage

Shamus and Murphy fancied a pint or two but didn't have a lot of money between them; they could only raise the staggering sum of one Euro.

Murphy said "Hang on, I have an idea."

He went next door to the butcher's shop and came out with one large sausage.

Shamus said "Are you crazy? Now we don't have any money left at all!"

Murphy replied, "Don't worry - just follow me."

He went into the pub where he immediately ordered two pints of Guinness and two glasses of Jameson Whisky.

Shamus said "Now you've lost it. Do you know how much trouble we will be in? We haven't got any money!!"

Murphy replied, with a smile. "Don't worry, I have a plan, Cheers!"

They downed their Drinks. Murphy said, "OK, I'll stick the sausage through my zipper and you go on your knees and put it in your mouth."

The barman noticed them, went berserk, and threw them out.

They continued this, pub after pub, getting more and more drunk, all for free.

At the tenth pub Shamus said "Murphy - I don't think I can do any more of this. I'm drunk and me knees are killin'me!"

Murphy said, "How do you think I feel?

I lost the sausage in the third pub.

Subject: Nurses aren't supposed to laugh.......

"Of course I won't laugh," said the nurse. "I'm a professional. In over twenty years I've never laughed at a patient."

"Okay then," said Fred, and he proceeded to drop his trousers, revealing the tiniest 'man thingy' the nurse had ever seen. Length and width, it couldn't have been bigger than an AAA battery.

Unable to control herself, the nurse started giggling, then fell to the floor laughing. Five minutes later she was able to struggle to her feet and regain her composure.

"I am so sorry," she said. "I don't know what came over me. On my honour as a nurse and a lady, I promise it won't happen again. Now, tell me, what seems to be the problem?"

"It's swollen," Fred replied.

She ran out of the room.

Subject: THE OLD MAN

An older man approached an attractive young woman at a shopping mall. 'Excuse me; I can't seem to find my wife. Can you talk to me for a couple of minutes?'

The woman, feeling a bit of compassion for the old fellow, said, 'Of course, sir. Do you know where your wife might be?'

'I have no idea, but every time I talk to a young woman with big tits, she appears out of nowhere.'

Subject: Irish Tradition

Paddy had long heard the stories of an amazing family tradition.

It seems that his father, grandfather and great-grandfather had all been able to walk on water on their 18th birthday. On that special day, they'd each walked across the lake to the pub on the far side for their first legal drink.

So when Paddy's, 18th birthday came 'round, he and his pal Mick, took a boat out to the middle of the lake, Paddy, stepped out of the boat ...and nearly drowned! Mick just barely managed to pull him to safety.

Furious and confused, Paddy, went to see his grandmother.

'Grandma,' he asked, "Tis me 18th birthday, so why can't I walk 'cross the lake like me father, his father, and his father before him?"

Granny looked deeply into Paddy's, troubled brown eyes and said, "Because ye father, ye grandfather and ye great-grandfather were all born in December, when the lake is frozen, and ye were born in August, ya fookin idiot!"

Subject: Last night

A Frenchman and an Italian were seated next to an Irishman on an overseas flight. After a few cocktails, the men began discussing their home lives.

"Last night I made love to my wife four times," the Frenchman bragged, "and this morning she made me delicious crepes and she told me how much she adored me."

"Ah, last night I made love to my wife six times," the Italian responded" and this morning she made me a wonderful omelette and told me she could never love another man."

When the Irishman remained silent, the Frenchman smugly asked, "And how many times did you make love to your wife last night?"

"Once," he replied.

"Only once?" the Italian arrogantly snorted. "And what did she say to you this morning?"

"Get off."

Subject: Theoretically v Realistically

A small boy says to his father "Dad, what's the difference between 'theoretically' and 'realistically'?"

His dad thinks and says "Right son, go and ask your mother if she'd sleep with Wayne Rooney for a million quid."

The boy toddles off and comes back saying "Dad, dad, she said she would! She would sleep with Wayne Rooney for a million pounds."

"OK son," says his dad. "Now go and ask your sister the same question."

The boy toddles off, and comes back saying "Dad, dad, she said she would too!"

So then his dad says "Right, son, now go and ask your brother if he'd sleep with Wayne Rooney for a million pounds."

The son comes back excitedly saying "Dad! Dad! He said he would too!"

"Well there you have it, son," said his dad.

Theoretically we could be sitting on three million quid.

Realistically we're living with two tarts and a poof."

There is the story of a pastor who got up one Sunday and announced to his congregation: "I have good news and bad news. The good news is, we have enough money to pay for our new building program. The bad news is, it's still out there in your pockets."

Subject: Be Strong

A man escapes from prison where he has been for 15 years. He breaks into a house to look for money and guns and finds a young couple in bed.

He orders the guy out of bed and ties him to a chair, while tying the girl to the bed he gets on top of her, kisses her neck, then gets up and goes into the bathroom.

While he's in there, the husband tells his wife: "Listen, this guy's an escaped convict, look at his clothes! He probably spent lots of time in jail and hasn't seen a woman in years. I saw how he kissed your neck." If he wants sex, don't resist, don't complain, do whatever he tells you. Satisfy him no matter how much he nauseates you. This guy is probably very dangerous. If he gets angry, he'll kill us. Be strong, honey. I love you."

To which his wife responds: "He wasn't kissing my neck. He was whispering in my ear. He told me he was gay, thought you were cute, and asked me if we had any Vaseline. I told him it was in the bathroom. Be strong honey.

I love you too!!"

Wedding Invite

YOU ARE REGRETFULLY INVITED
TO THE WEDDING BETWEEN MY PERFECT SON,

The Doctor

AND SOME

Cheap Two-Bit Tramp

WHOSE NAME ESCAPES ME RIGHT NOW.

THE BIGGEST DISASTER IN MY
FAMILY'S HISTORY WILL TAKE PLACE AT

9pm on Saturday, September 8th

AND NO DOUBT END IN DIVORCE.
HOPEFULLY IN TIME TO STILL BE ELIGIBLE FOR AN ANNULMENT.
THE OVERWHELMINGLY DISAPPOINTING HEARTBREAK OF A CEREMONY
WILL BE FOLLOWED BY DINNER, WHERE NUTS WILL BE SERVED
BECAUSE WHATSHERFACE HAS AN ALLERGY.

Subject: FW: A PRE-SCHOOL TEST FOR YOU

I already knew I was thicker than 11 year olds ... but now it's the pre-schoolers??
Which way is the bus below travelling?
To the left or to the right?

Can't make up your mind?
Look carefully at the picture again.
Still don't know?
Pre-schoolers all over the United Kingdom were shown this picture and
asked the same question.
90% of the pre-schoolers gave this answer.
"The bus is travelling to the right."
When asked, "Why do you think the bus is travelling to the right?"

They answered: "Because you can't see the door to get on the bus."
How do you feel now???

(Reverse this for American & European readers)

Subject: UNDERSTANDING ENGINEERS

Understanding Engineers 1

Two engineering students were cycling across a university campus when one said, "Where did you get such a great bike?"

The second engineer replied, "Well, I was walking along yesterday, minding my own business, when a beautiful young woman rode up on this bike, threw it to the ground, took off all her clothes and said, "Take what you want."

The first engineer nodded approvingly and said, "Good choice; the clothes wouldn't fit you anyway."

Understanding Engineers 2

To the optimist, the glass is half-full.

To the pessimist, the glass is half-empty.

To the engineer, the glass is twice as big as it needs to be.

Understanding Engineers 3

A priest, a doctor, and an engineer were waiting one morning for a particularly slow group of golfers. The engineer fumed, "What's with those guys? We must have been waiting for fifteen minutes!"

The doctor chimed in, "I don't know, but I've never seen such inept golf!"

The priest said, "Here comes the green-keeper. Let's have a word."

He said, "Hello George, what's wrong with that group ahead of us? They're rather slow, aren't they?" The green-keeper replied, "Oh, yes. That's a group of blind firemen. They lost their sight saving our clubhouse last year, so we always let them play for free."

The group fell silent for a moment.

The priest said, "That's so sad. I will say a special prayer for them."

The doctor said, "Good idea. I'm going to contact my ophthalmologist colleague and see if there's anything he can do for them."

The engineer said, "Why can't they play at night?"

Understanding Engineers 4

What is the difference between mechanical engineers and civil engineers?

Mechanical engineers build weapons.

Civil engineers build targets.

Understanding Engineers 5

The graduate with a science degree asks, "Why does it work?"

The graduate with an accounting degree asks, "How much will it cost?"

The graduate with an engineering degree asks, "How does it work?"

The graduate with an arts degree asks, "Do you want fries with that?"

Understanding Engineers 6

Three engineering students were gathered together discussing who must have designed the human body.

One said, "It was a mechanical engineer. Just look at all the joints."

Another said, "No, it was an electrical engineer. The nervous system has many thousands of electrical connections." The last one said, "No, actually it had to have been a civil engineer. Who else would run a toxic waste pipeline through a recreational area?

In a London Laundromat:

AUTOMATIC WASHING MACHINES:
PLEASE REMOVE ALL YOUR CLOTHES WHEN THE LIGHT GOES OUT.

These are sentences exactly as typed by medical secretaries in NHS Greater Glasgow

1. The patient has no previous history of suicide.
2. Patient has left her white blood cells at another hospital.
3. Patient's medical history has been remarkably insignificant with only a 40 pound weight gain in the past three days.
4. She has no rigors or shaking chills, but her husband states she was very hot in bed last night.
5. Patient has chest pain if she lies on her left side for over a year.
6. On the second day the knee was better and on the third day it disappeared.
7. She is constantly tearful and crying. She also appears to be depressed.
8. The patient has been depressed since she began seeing me in 1993.
9. Discharge status: - Alive, but without my permission.
10. Healthy, appearing decrepit 69-year old male, mentally alert, but forgetful.
11. Patient had waffles for breakfast and anorexia for lunch.
12. She is numb from her toes down.
13. While in ER, she was examined, x-rated and sent home.
14. The skin was moist and dry.
15. Occasional, constant infrequent headaches.
16. Patient was alert and unresponsive.
17. Rectal examination revealed a normal size thyroid.
18. She had been constipated for most of her life until she got a divorce.
19. I saw your patient today, who is still under our care for physical therapy.
20. Both breasts are equal and reactive to light and accommodation.
21. Examination of genitalia reveals that he is circus sized.
22. The lab test indicated abnormal lover function.
23. Skin: somewhat pale, but present.
24. The pelvic exam will be done later on the floor.

25. Large brown stool ambulating in the hall.
26. Patient has two teenage children, but no other abnormalities.
27. When she fainted, her eyes rolled around the room.
28. The patient was in his usual state of good health until his airplane ran out of fuel and crashed.
29. Between you and me, we ought to be able to get this lady pregnant.
30. She slipped on the ice and apparently her legs went in separate directions in early December.
31. Patient was seen in consultation by Dr. Smith, who felt we should sit on the abdomen and I agree.
32. The patient was to have a bowel resection. However, he took a job as a stock broker instead.

Subject: No one believes

An elderly couple was celebrating their sixtieth anniversary. The couple had married as childhood sweethearts and had moved back to their old neighbourhood after they retired. Holding hands, they walked back to their old school. It was not locked, so they entered, and found the old desk they'd shared, where Andy had carved "I love you, Sally."

On their way back home, a bag of money fell out of an armoured car, landing at their feet. Sally quickly picked it up and, not sure what to do with it, they took it home. There, she counted the money - fifty thousand dollars!

Andy said, "We've got to give it back."

Sally said, "Finders keepers." She put the money back in the bag and hid it in their attic.

The next day, two police officers were canvassing the neighbourhood looking for the money, and knocked on their door. "Pardon me, did either of you find a bag that fell out of an armoured car yesterday?"

Sally said, "No".

Andy said, "She's lying. She hid it up in the attic.

Sally said, "Don't believe him, he's getting senile"

The agents turned to Andy and began to question him. One said: "Tell us the story from the beginning."

Andy said, "Well, when Sally and I were walking home from school yesterday "

The first police officer turned to his partner and said, "We're outta here!"

If you want breakfast in bed, then start sleeping in the kitchen.

Subject: THE STRANGER IN OUR HOUSE

A few years after I was born, my Dad met a stranger who was new to our small Texas town. From the beginning, Dad was fascinated with this enchanting newcomer and soon invited him to live with our family. The stranger was quickly accepted and was around from then on.

As I grew up, I never questioned his place in my family. In my young mind, he had a special niche. My parents were complementary instructors: Mom taught me good from evil, and Dad taught me to obey. But the stranger...he was our storyteller. He would keep us spellbound for hours on end with adventures, mysteries and comedies.

If I wanted to know anything about politics, history or science, he always knew the answers about the past, understood the present and even seemed able to predict the future! He took my family to the first major league ball game. He made me laugh, and he made me cry. The stranger never stopped talking, but Dad didn't seem to mind.

Sometimes, Mom would get up quietly while the rest of us were shushing each other to listen to what he had to say, and she would go to the kitchen for peace and quiet. (I wonder now if she ever prayed for the stranger to leave.)

Dad ruled our household with certain moral convictions, but the stranger never felt obligated to honour them. Profanity, for example, was not allowed in our home... Not from us, our friends or any visitors. Our long-time visitor, however, got away with four-letter words that burned my ears and made my dad squirm and my mother blush. My Dad didn't permit the liberal use of alcohol. But the stranger encouraged us to try it on a regular basis. He made cigarettes look cool, cigars manly and pipes distinguished.

He talked freely (much too freely!) about sex. His comments were sometimes blatant, sometimes suggestive, and generally embarrassing. I now know that my early concepts about relationships were influenced strongly by the stranger. Time after time, he opposed the values of my parents, yet he was seldom rebuked... And NEVER asked to leave.

More than fifty years have passed since the stranger moved in with our family. He has blended right in and is not nearly as fascinating as he was at first. Still, if you could walk into my parents' den today, you would still find him sitting over in his corner, waiting for someone to listen to him talk and watch him draw his pictures.

His name?....

We just call him 'TV.'

He has a wife now...We call her 'Computer.'

Oak trees do not produce acorns until they are fifty (50) years of age or older.

Subject: 5 Minute Management Course

Lesson 1:

A man is getting into the shower just as his wife is finishing up her shower, when the doorbell rings.

The wife quickly wraps herself in a towel and runs downstairs.

When she opens the door, there stands Bob, the next-door neighbour.

Before she says a word, Bob says: 'I'll give you $800 to drop that towel'

After thinking for a moment, the woman drops her towel and stands naked in front of Bob, after a few seconds, Bob hands her $800 and leaves.

The woman wraps back up in the towel and goes back upstairs.

When she gets to the bathroom, her husband asks: 'Who was that?'

'It was Bob the next door neighbour' she replies.

'Great' the husband says, 'did he say anything about the $800 he owes me?'

Moral of the story:

If you share critical information pertaining to credit and risk with your shareholders, in time, you may be in a position to prevent avoidable exposure.

Lesson 2:

A priest offered a Nun a lift.

She got in and crossed her legs, forcing her gown to reveal a leg.

The priest nearly had an accident.

After controlling the car, he stealthily slid his hand up her leg.

The nun said, 'Father, remember Psalm 129.'

The priest removed his hand, but, changing gears, he let his hand slide up her leg again.

The nun once again said, 'Father, remember Psalm 129.'

The priest apologized 'Sorry sister but the flesh is weak'

Arriving at the convent, the nun sighed heavily and went on her way.

On his arrival at the church, the priest rushed to look up Psalm 129.

It said, 'Go forth and seek, further up, you will find glory'.

Moral of the story:

If you are not well informed in your job, you might miss a great opportunity.

Lesson 3:

A sales rep, an administration clerk, and the manager are walking to lunch when they find an antique oil lamp. They rub it and a Genie comes out.
The Genie says, 'I'll give each of you just one wish'.
'Me first! Me first!' says the admin clerk. 'I want to be in the Bahamas, driving a speedboat, without a care in the world'.   Puff! She's gone.
'Me next! Me next!' says the sales rep. 'I want to be in Hawaii, relaxing on the beach with my personal masseuse, an endless supply of Pina Coladas and the love of my life'.   Puff! He's gone.
'OK, you're up,' the Genie says to the manager.
The manager says, 'I want those two back in the office after lunch'.

Moral of the story:
Always let your boss have the first say.

Lesson 4

An eagle was sitting on a tree resting, doing nothing.
A small rabbit saw the eagle and asked him, 'Can I also sit like you and do nothing?
The eagle answered: 'Sure, why not.'
So, the rabbit sat on the ground below the eagle and rested. All of a sudden, a fox appeared, jumped on the rabbit and ate it.

Moral of the story:
To be sitting and doing nothing, you must be sitting very, very high up.

Lesson 5

A turkey was chatting with a bull. 'I would love to be able to get to the top of that tree' sighed the turkey, 'but I haven't got the energy'.
'Well, why don't you nibble on some of my droppings?' replied the bull. They're packed with nutrients'.
The turkey pecked at a lump of dung, and found it actually gave him enough strength to reach the lowest branch of the tree.
The next day, after eating some more dung, he reached the second branch.
Finally after a fourth night, the turkey was proudly perched at the top of the tree He was promptly spotted by a farmer, who shot him out of the tree.

Moral of the story:
Bull Shit might get you to the top, but it won't keep you there.

Lesson 6

A little bird was flying south for the winter. It was so cold the bird froze and fell to the ground into a large field.

While he was lying there, a cow came by and dropped some dung on him...

As the frozen bird lay there in the pile of cow dung, he began to realize how warm he was.

The dung was actually thawing him out!

He lay there all warm and happy, and soon began to sing for joy.

A passing cat heard the bird singing and came to investigate.

Following the sound, the cat discovered the bird under the pile of cow dung, and promptly dug him out and ate him.

Morals of the story:

(1) Not everyone who shits on you is your enemy.

(2) Not everyone who gets you out of shit is your friend.

(3) And when you're in deep shit, it's best to keep your mouth shut!

THUS ENDS THE FIVE MINUTE MANAGEMENT COURSE

Subject: My darling husband,

Before you return from your trip I just want to let you know about the small accident I had with the car when I turned into our driveway.

Fortunately it's not too bad and I really didn't get hurt, so please don't worry too much about me.

I was coming home from town and when I turned into the driveway I accidentally pushed down on the accelerator instead of the brake.

The garage door is slightly bent but the car fortunately came to a halt when it bumped into *your* new car.

I am really sorry, but I know with your kind-hearted personality you will forgive me. You know how much I love you and care for you my sweetheart. I am enclosing a picture for you. I cannot wait to hold you in my arms again.

Your loving wife.

P.S.

Your girlfriend phoned.

Subject: FROM THE JUNGLE

A Priest was about to finish his tour of duty, and was leaving his Mission.

In the jungle, where he has spent years teaching the natives, when he realizes that the one thing he never taught them was how to speak English.

So he takes the chief for a walk in the forest. He points to a tree and says to the chief, "This is a tree."

The chief looks at the tree and grunts, "Tree."

The Priest is pleased with the response. They walk a little further and he points to a rock and says, "This is a rock."

Hearing this, the chief looks and grunts, Rock.'

The Priest was really getting enthusiastic about the results when he hears a rustling in the bushes. As they peek over the top, he sees a couple of natives in the midst of heavy sexual activity.

The Priest is really flustered and quickly responds, "Man riding a bike."

The chief looks at the couple briefly, pulls out his blowgun and kills them.

The Priest goes ballistic and yells at the chief that he has spent years teaching the tribe how to be civilized and be kind to each other, so how could he kill these people in cold blood that way?

The chief replied, "My bike."

THE LEATHER DRESS

Do you know that when a woman wears a leather dress, a man's heart beats quicker, his throat gets dry, he gets weak in the knees and he begins to think irrationally?

Ever wonder why?

It's because she smells like a new car!

Murphy arrived home late from the pub, well oiled and ready for trouble. "Is that you Murphy?" called his wife. "Byjasis! It damned well better be!"

PADDY... "If you can guess how many chickens I have in my bag, you can have both of them."   **"Three?"**... Suggested Shaun.

If the cops arrest a mime do they tell him that he has the right to remain silent?

Subject: The Glasgow Brothel

The madam opened the brothel door in Glasgow and saw a rather dignified, well-dressed, good-looking man in his late forties or early fifties.

"May I help you sir?" she asked.

"I want to see Valerie," the man replied.

"Sir, Valerie is one of our most expensive ladies. Perhaps you would prefer someone else", said the madam.

"No, I must see Valerie," he replied.

Just then, Valerie appeared and announced to the man she charged £5000 a visit. Without hesitation, the man pulled out five thousand pounds and gave it to Valerie, and they went upstairs. After an hour, the man calmly left.

The next night, the man appeared again, once more demanding to see Valerie. Valerie explained that no one had ever come back two nights in a row, as she was so expensive. There were no discounts. The price was still £5000.

Again, the man pulled out the money, gave it to Valerie, and they went upstairs. After an hour, he left.

The following night the man was there yet again. Everyone was astounded that he had come for a third consecutive night, but he paid Valerie and they went upstairs. After their session, Valerie said to the man, "No one has ever been with me three nights in a row. Where are you from?"

The man replied, "Edinburgh."

"Really", she said. "I have family in Edinburgh."

"I know." the man said. "Your sister died, and I'm her solicitor. I was instructed to deliver your £15,000 inheritance in person."

The moral of the story is that three things in life are certain................

1. Death
2. Taxes
3. Being screwed by a lawyer

My sister and I were at the mall and passed by a store that sold a variety of candy and nuts.
As we were looking at the display case, the boy behind the counter asked if we needed any help.
I replied, "No, I'm just looking at your nuts."
My sister started to laugh hysterically and I just had to run out of the store.

I almost had a psychic girlfriend but she left me before we met

Subject: The Haircut

One day a florist went to a barber for a haircut. After the cut, he asked about his bill, and the barber replied, 'I cannot accept money from you; I'm doing community service this week.' The florist was pleased and left the shop. When the barber went to open his shop the next morning, there was a 'thank you' card and a dozen roses waiting for him at his door.

Later, a cop comes in for a haircut, and when he tries to pay his bill, the barber again replied, 'I cannot accept money from you; I'm doing community service this week.' The cop was happy and left the shop. The next morning when the barber went to open up, there was a 'thank you' card and a dozen donuts waiting for him at his door?

Then a Member of Parliament came in for a haircut, and when he went to pay his bill, the barber again replied, 'I cannot accept money from you. I'm doing community service this week.' The Member of Parliament was very happy and left the shop. The next morning, when the barber went to open up, there were a dozen other Members of Parliament lined up waiting for a free haircut.

And that, my friends, illustrates the fundamental difference between the citizens of our country, and the politicians who run it!

Subject: A tragedy!!??

Martin McGuinness[11] is visiting a primary school and he visits one of the classes. They are in the middle of a discussion related to words and their meanings. The teacher asks the visitor if he would like to lead the discussion on the word "tragedy".

So the illustrious Deputy First Minister asks for an example of a "tragedy".

One little boy stands up and offers: "If my best friend, who lives on a farm, is playing in the field and a bad man comes along and knocks him dead with a log, that would be a tragedy."

"No," says Martin McGuinness," that would be an accident."

A little girl raises her hand: "If a school bus carrying 50 children drove over a cliff, killing everyone inside, that would be a tragedy."

"I'm afraid not," explains the Minister. "That's what we call a great loss."

The room goes silent. No other children volunteer.

Martin searches the room. "Isn't there someone here who can give me an example of a tragedy?"

Finally at the back of the room a small boy raises his hand. In a quiet voice he says: "If a private jet carrying Gerry Adams and Martin McGuinness were struck by a missile and blown to smithereens that would be a tragedy."

"Fantastic!" exclaims the Minister, "That's right. And can you tell me why that would be tragedy?"

"Well," says the boy, "because it certainly wouldn't be a great loss and it probably wouldn't be an accident either.

Subject: A Blonde's Snow Day

Norman and his blonde wife live in Prince George, Canada.
One winter morning while listening to the radio, they hear the announcer say, "We are going to have 3 to 4 inches of snow today. You must park your car on the even numbered side of the street, so the snowplough can get through."
Norman's wife goes out and moves her car.
A week later while they are eating breakfast, the radio announcer says, "We are expecting 4 to 5 inches of snow today. You must park your car on the odd numbered side of the street, so the snowplough can get through."
Norman's wife goes out and moves her car again.
The next week they are having breakfast again, when the announcer says "We are expecting 10 to 12 inches of snow today. You must park...??" then the electric power goes out.
Norman's wife says, "Honey, I don't know what to do."
Norman says, "Why don't you just leave it in the garage this time?"

Subject: The Old Man

A woman walks up to an old man sitting in a chair on his porch. "I couldn't help but notice how happy you look," she said. "What's your secret for a long, happy life?" "I smoke three packs of cigarettes a day, drink a case of beer, eat fatty foods, and never, ever exercise," he replied. "Wow, that's amazing," she said, "How old are you?"   -
"Twenty-six."

Subject: DIVORCE VS. MURDER

A nice, calm and respectable lady went into the pharmacy, walked up to the pharmacist, looked straight into his eyes, and said, "I would like to buy some cyanide."
The pharmacist asked, "Why in the world do you need cyanide?"
The lady replied, "I need it to poison my husband."
The pharmacist's eyes got big and he explained, "Lord have mercy! I can't give you cyanide to kill your husband, that's against the law? I'll lose my licence! They'll throw both of us in jail! All kinds of bad things will happen. Absolutely not! You CANNOT have any cyanide!"
The lady reached into her purse and pulled out a picture of her husband in bed with the pharmacist's wife.
The pharmacist looked at the picture and replied,
"You didn't tell me you had a prescription."

Subject: CATHOLIC SCHOOL

Until a child tells you what they are thinking, we can't even begin to imagine how their mind is working. Little Zachary was doing very badly in math. His parents had tried everything...tutors, mentors, flash cards, special learning centres. In short, everything they could think of to help his math. Finally, in a last ditch effort, they took Zachary down and enrolled him in the local Catholic school. After the first day, little Zachary came home with a very serious look on his face. He didn't even kiss his mother hello. Instead, he went straight to his room and started studying. Books and papers were spread out all over the room and little Zachary was hard at work. His mother was amazed. She called him down to dinner. To her shock, the minute he was done, he marched back to his room without a word, and in no time, he was back hitting the books as hard as before. This went on for some time, day after day, while the mother tried to understand what made all the difference.

Finally, little Zachary brought home his report card. He quietly laid it on the table, went up to his room and hit the books. With great trepidation, His Mom looked at it and to her great surprise; Zachary got an 'A' in math. She could no longer hold her curiosity. She went to his room and said, 'Son, what was it? Was it the nuns?' Little Zachary looked at her and shook his head, no.. 'Well, then,' she replied, was it the books, the discipline, the structure, the uniforms? WHAT WAS IT?'

Little Zachary looked at her and said, 'Well, on the first day of school when I saw that guy nailed to the plus sign, I knew they weren't fooling around.'

Subject: Lunchtime

An old nun who was living in a convent next to a construction site noticed the coarse language of the workers and decided to spend some time with them to correct their ways. She decided she would take her lunch; sit with the workers; and talk with them.

She put her sandwich in a brown bag and walked over to the spot where the men were eating. With a big smile, she walked up to the group and asked: "And do you men know Jesus Christ?"

They shook their heads and looked at each other.... very confused.

One of the workers looked up into the steelworks and yelled out, "Anybody up there know Jesus Christ?"

One of the steelworkers yelled down, "Why?"

The worker yelled back,

"'Cause his wife's here with his lunch."

Subject: PADDY AGAIN

Paddy calls the airline to book a flight. The operator asks 'How many people are flying with you?'
Paddy replies 'I don't know! You should know. It's your plane!!'

Two Irish couples decided to swap partners for the night. After 3 hours of amazing sex Paddy says 'I wonder how the girls are getting on.'

Paddy the electrician got sacked from the U.S. prison service for not servicing the electric chair. He said in his professional opinion it was a death trap!

Paddy & his wife are lying in bed & the neighbour's dog is barking like mad in their garden. Paddy says 'To hell with this!' & storms off.
He comes back upstairs 5 minutes later & his wife asks 'What did you do?'
Paddy replies - I've put the dog in _our_ garden, let's see how _they_ like it!'

Mick & Paddy are reading head stones at a nearby cemetery. Mick says 'Crikey! There's a bloke here who was 52!'
Paddy says 'What's his name?'
Mick replies 'Miles from London

SUBJECT: At St. Peter's Catholic Church in New York City, they have weekly husband's marriage seminars.

At the session last week, the priest asked Giuseppe, who said he was approaching his 50th wedding anniversary, to take a few minutes and share some insight into how he had managed to stay married to the same woman all these years.
Giuseppe replied to the assembled husbands,
 'Wella, I'va tried to treat her nicea, spenda da money on her, but besta of all is, I tooka her to Italy for the 25th anniversary! '
The priest responded,
'Giuseppe, you are an amazing inspiration to all the husbands here! Please tell us what you are planning for your wife for your 50th anniversary? '
Giuseppe proudly replied,
"I gonna go pick her up."

In Shakespeare's time, mattresses were secured on bed frames by ropes.
When you pulled on the ropes, the mattress tightened, making the bed firmer to sleep on.
Hence the phrase...'Goodnight, sleep tight'

Subject: The New Bride

A new bride was a bit embarrassed to be known as a honeymooner. So when she and her husband pulled up to the hotel, she asked him if there was any way that they could make it appear that they had been married a long time. He responded, "Sure. You carry the suitcases!"

Subject: There was a man who worked for the Post Office whose job was to process all the mail that had illegible addresses.

One day, a letter came addressed in a shaky handwriting to God with no actual address. He thought he should open it to see what it was about.

The letter read:

Dear God,

I am an 83 year old widow, living on a very small pension.

Yesterday someone stole my purse. It had £100 in it, which was all the money I had until my next pension payment.

Next Sunday is Christmas, and I had invited two of my friends over for dinner. Without that money, I have nothing to buy food with, have no family to turn to, and you are my only hope.. Can you please help me?

Sincerely, Edna

The postal worker was touched.. He showed the letter to all the other workers. Each one dug into his or her wallet and came up with a few pounds.

By the time he made the rounds, he had collected £96, which they put into an envelope and sent to the woman.

The rest of the day, all the workers felt a warm glow thinking of Edna and the dinner she would be able to share with her friends.

Christmas came and went. A few days later, another letter came from the same old lady to God.

All the workers gathered around while the letter was opened.

It read:

Dear God,

How can I ever thank you enough for what you did for me?

Because of your gift of love, I was able to fix a glorious dinner for my friends. We had a very nice day and I told my friends of your wonderful gift.

By the way, there was £4 missing.

I think it might have been those b***ds down at the post office.**

Sincerely, Edna

Q. Where do you get virgin wool from?
A. Ugly sheep.

Subject: Teachers & Educators

According to a news report, a certain private school in Newcastle Upon Tyne[12] was recently faced with a unique problem.

A number of 12-year-old girls were beginning to use lipstick and would put it on in the bathroom.

That was fine, but after they put on their lipstick they would press their lips to the mirror leaving dozens of little lip prints.

Every night the maintenance man would remove them and the next day the girls would put them back.

Finally the Headmistress decided that something had to be done.

She called all the girls to the bathroom and met them there with the maintenance man.

She explained that all these lip prints were causing a major problem for the custodian who had to clean the mirrors every night. To demonstrate how difficult it had been to clean the mirrors, she asked the maintenance man to show the girls how much effort was required.

He took out a long-handled squeegee, dipped it in the toilet, and cleaned the mirror with it.

Since then, there have been no lip prints on the mirror.

There are teachers....... .and then there are educators.

Subject: THE NEVER ENDING SOAP OPERA OF MARGARET & BERT

Bert always wanted a pair of authentic cowboy boots, so, seeing some on sale, he bought them and wore them home.

Walking proudly, he sauntered into the kitchen and said to his wife, "Notice anything different about me?"

Margaret looked him over. "Nope.

Frustrated, Bert stormed off into the bathroom, undressed and walked back into the kitchen completely naked except for the boots.

Again he asked Margaret, a little louder this time, "Notice anything different **NOW?**"

Margaret looked up and said in her best deadpan, "Bert, what's different? It's hanging down today, it was hanging down yesterday, and it'll be hanging down again tomorrow."

Furious, Bert yelled,

"AND DO YOU KNOW WHY IT'S HANGING DOWN, MARGARET?"

"Nope. Not a clue", she replied.

"IT'S HANGING DOWN, BECAUSE IT'S LOOKING AT MY NEW BOOTS!!!!"

Without missing a beat Margaret replied,

"Shoulda bought a hat, Bert. Shoulda bought a hat."

Acupuncture: - a **jab** well done?

Subject: Three dead bodies turn up at the mortuary,

all with very big smiles on their faces. The coroner calls the police to tell them what has happened.

Coroner tells the Inspector:

'First body: An Italian, 60, died of heart failure while with his Mistress hence the enormous smile.'

'Second body: Scotsman, 25, won a thousand pounds on the lottery, spent it all on whisky, died of alcohol poisoning, hence the smile.'

The Inspector asked, 'What of the third body?'

'Ah.' says the coroner, 'This is the most unusual one. Billy Earl, the Irishman, 30, struck by lightning.'

'Why is he smiling then?' inquires the Inspector.

'Thought he was having his picture taken!'

A policeman pulled a blonde over after she'd been driving the wrong way on a one-way street.

Cop: Do you know where you were going?

Blonde: No, but wherever it is, it must be bad because all the cars were leaving.

Like the Irish patient who hobbled into the Surgery's' waiting room. "I hope to God the doctor finds something wrong with me because I'd hate to feel like this, if I was well!"

Subject: THE HELPFUL HUSBAND

When our lawn mower broke and wouldn't run, my wife kept hinting to me that I should get it fixed.

But, somehow I always had something else to take care of first, the shed, the boat, making beer. Always something more important to me. Finally she thought of a clever way to make her point.

When I arrived home one day, I found her seated in the tall grass, busily snipping away with a tiny pair of sewing scissors. I watched silently for a short time and then went into the house.. I was gone only a minute, and when I came out again I handed her a toothbrush. I said, "When you finish cutting the grass, you might as well sweep the driveway."

The doctors say I will walk again, but I will always have a limp.

My girlfriend thinks that I'm a stalker. Well, she's not exactly my girlfriend yet.

Subject: An old German Shepherd Dog

Starts chasing rabbits and before long, discovers that he's lost. Wandering about, he notices a panther heading rapidly in his direction with the intention of having lunch.

The old German Shepherd thinks, "Oh, oh! I'm in deep doo doo now!" Noticing some bones on the ground close by, he immediately settles down to chew on the bones with his back to the approaching cat. Just as the panther is about to leap, the old German Shepherd exclaims loudly, "Boy, that was one delicious panther! I wonder, if there are any more around here?"

Hearing this, the young panther halts his attack in mid-strike, a look of terror comes over him and he slinks away into the trees.

"Whew!," says the panther, "That was close! That old German Shepherd nearly had me!"

Meanwhile, a squirrel who had been watching the whole scene from a nearby tree, figures he can put this knowledge to good use and trade it for protection from the panther. So, off he goes.

The squirrel soon catches up with the panther, spills the beans and strikes a deal for himself with the panther.

The young panther is furious at being made a fool of and says, "Here, squirrel, hop on my back and see what's going to happen to that conniving canine!"

Now, the old German Shepherd sees the panther coming with the squirrel on his back and thinks, "What am I going to do now?," but instead of running, the dog sits down with his back to his attackers, pretending he hasn't seen them yet, and just when they get close enough to hear, the old German Shepherd says...

"Where's that squirrel? I sent him off an hour ago to bring me another panther!"

Moral of this story -

Don't mess with the old dogs... Age and skill will always overcome youth and treachery!

Your glass is empty O'Flaherty, will you be having another?"
"And why would I be wanting two empty glasses?" replied O'Flaherty.

A Chinese man is making love to his wife. He whispers in her ear, Baby, I wanna 69.
*She gives him a strange look and replies, "You want King prawn flied lice **now**"*

Subject: The Hotel Bill

An elderly lady decided to give herself a big treat for a significant birthday by staying overnight in one of London's most expensive hotels.

When she checked out next morning, the desk clerk handed her a bill for £250.00.

She exploded and demanded to know why the charge was so high. "It's a nice hotel but the rooms certainly aren't worth £250.00 for just an overnight stop, without even breakfast."

The clerk told her that £250.00 is the 'standard rate' so she insisted on speaking to the Manager.

The Manager appeared and forewarned by the desk clerk announced:
 "The hotel has an Olympic-sized pool and a huge conference centre which are available for use."

'But I didn't use them," she said,

"Well, they are here, and you could have," explained the Manager. He went on to explain that she could also have seen one of the in-hotel shows for which the hotel is famous.

"We have the best entertainers from London, Edinburgh, Glasgow, and Aberdeen performing here" the Manager said.

"But I didn't go to any of those shows," she said

The Manager was unmoved, so she decided to pay, wrote a cheque and gave it to the Manager. The Manager was surprised when he looked at the cheque. "But madam, this cheque is only made out for £50.00."

'That's correct. I charged you £200.00 for sleeping with me," she replied.

"But I didn't!" exclaims the very surprised Manager.

"Well, too bad, I was here, available and you could have."

Don't mess with Senior Citizens

Subject: ORIGIN OF THE WHITE WEDDING DRESS

A son asked his mother the following question:

'Mom, why are wedding dresses white?'

The mother looks at her son and replies:

'Son, this shows your friends and relatives that your bride is pure.'

The son thanks his Mom and goes off to double-check this with his father.

'Dad why are wedding dresses white?'

The father looks at his son in surprise and says:

'Son, all household appliances come in white.'

Subject: Bring back any memories?

Someone asked the other day, 'What was your favourite 'fast food' when you were growing up?'

'We didn't have fast food when I was growing up,' I informed him.

'All the food was slow.'

'C'mon, seriously. Where did you eat?'

'It was a place called 'home,' I explained!

'Mum cooked every day and when Dad got home from work, we sat down together at the dining room table, and if I didn't like what she put on my plate, I was allowed to sit there until I did like it.'

By this time, the lad was laughing so hard I was afraid he was going to suffer serious internal damage, so I didn't tell him the part about how I had to have permission to leave the table.

But here are some other things I would have told him about my childhood if I'd figured his system could have handled it:

Some parents NEVER owned their own house, wore jeans, set foot on a golf course, travelled out of the country or had a credit card.

My parents never drove me to school. I had a bicycle that weighed probably 50 pounds, and only had one speed, (slow).

We didn't have a television in our house until I was 10. It was, of course, black and white, and the station went off the air at 10 pm, after playing the national anthem and epilogue; it came back on the air at about 6 a.m. and there was usually a local news and farm show on, featuring local people.

I never had a telephone in my room. The only phone was on a party line. Before you could dial, you had to listen and make sure some people you didn't know weren't already using the line.

Pizzas were not delivered to our home. But milk was. All newspapers were delivered by boys and all boys delivered newspapers. My brother delivered a newspaper, seven days a week. He had to get up at 6am every morning.

Film stars kissed with their mouths shut. At least, they did in the films. There were no movie ratings because all movies were responsibly produced for everyone to enjoy viewing, without profanity or violence or almost anything offensive. *If you grew up in a generation before there was fast food, you may want to share some of these memories with your children or grandchildren. Just don't blame me if they bust a gut laughing.*

Growing up isn't what it used to be, is it?

How do you make Holy Water? Boil the hell out of it.

Subject: The Sperm Count

An 85-year-old man was requested by his doctor for a sperm count as part of his physical exam.

The doctor gave the man a jar and said, "Take this jar home and bring back a semen sample tomorrow." The next day the 85-year-old man reappeared at the doctor's office and gave him the jar, which was as clean and empty as on the previous day.

The doctor asked, what happened and the man explained.

"Well, doc, it's like this--first I tried with my right hand, but nothing. Then I tried with my left hand, but still nothing. Then I asked my wife for help. She tried with her right hand, then with her left, still nothing. She tried with her mouth, first with the teeth in, then with her teeth out, still nothing. We even called up Arleen, the lady next door and she tried too, first with both hands, then an armpit, and she even tried squeezing it between her knees, but still nothing."

The doctor was shocked! "You asked your neighbour?"

The old man replied, **"Yep, none of us could get the jar open."**

Subject: A redhead, a brunette and a blonde

Robbed a supermarket. While the robbery was in progress, a police officer walked in the store and saw what was happening. He dashed toward them, but they were able to get away into the back of the store. There they found three sacks to hide in. When the police officer checked there, he examined each sack.

He kicks the first bag, and the redhead says "meow" in a high voice. The cop determines that it must only be a cat in that bag, and he moves on to the next.

When he kicks the second bag, the brunette says "woof" in a low voice. The officer determines that it must only be a dog in that bag, so he moves on to the last bag.

He kicks the third bag, and the blonde shouts "potato" to the officer.

To be happy with a man, you must understand him a lot and love him a little.

To be happy with a woman, you must love her a lot and not try to understand her at all.

Support bacteria - they're the only culture some people have

Fondling In Bed

After 20 years of marriage, a couple was lying in bed one evening, when the wife felt her husband begin to fondle her in ways he hadn't in quite some time.

It almost tickled as his fingers started at her neck, and then began moving down past the small of her back.

He then caressed her shoulders and neck, slowly worked his hand down over her breasts, stopping just over her lower stomach.

He then proceeded to place his hand on her left inner arm, caressed past the side of her breast again, working down her side, passed gently over her buttock and down her leg to her calf. Then, he proceeded up her inner thigh, stopping just at the uppermost portion of her leg. He continued in the same manner on her right side, then suddenly stopped, rolled over and started to watch the tv.

As she had become quite aroused by this caressing, she asked in a loving voice, "That was wonderful. Why did you stop?"

He said, "I found the remote".

ZEN TEACHINGS

1. Do not walk behind me, for I may not lead. Do not walk ahead of me, for I may not follow. Do not walk beside me for the path is narrow. In fact, just go away and leave me alone.
2. Sex is like air. It's not that important unless you aren't getting any.
3. No one is listening until you fart.
4. Always remember you're unique. Just like everyone else.
5. Never test the depth of the water with both feet.
6. If you think nobody cares whether you're alive or dead, try missing a couple of mortgage payments.
7. Before you criticize someone, you should walk a mile in their shoes. Then, when you criticize them, you're a mile away and have their shoes.
8. If at first you don't succeed, skydiving is not for you.
9. Give a man a fish and he will eat for a day. Teach him how to fish, and he will sit in a boat and drink beer all day.
10. If you lend someone £20 and never see that person again, it was probably well worth it.
11. If you tell the truth, you don't have to remember anything.
12. Some days you are the dog, some days you are the tree.
13. Don't worry; it only seems kinky the first time.
14. Good judgment comes from bad experience ... And most of that comes from bad judgment.
15. A closed mouth gathers no foot.
16. There are two excellent theories for arguing with women. Neither one works.
17. Generally speaking, you aren't learning much when your lips are moving.
18. Experience is something you don't get until just after you need it.
19. We are born naked, wet and hungry, and get slapped on our arse .... Then things just keep getting worse.
20. Never, under any circumstances, take a sleeping pill and a laxative on the same night.

Did you hear about the blonde who studied for her blood test and still failed it?

And did you hear about the blonde who tripped over her cordless phone?

Subject: Memories from a friend:

My Dad is cleaning out my grandmother's house (she died in December) and he brought me an old Woodroofe's Lemonade bottle. In the bottle top was a stopper with a bunch of holes in it... I knew immediately what it was, but my daughter had no idea. She thought they had tried to make it a salt shaker or something. I knew it as the bottle that sat on the end of the ironing board to 'sprinkle' clothes with because we didn't have steam irons. Man, I am old.

How many do you remember?

Headlight dip-switches on the floor of the car.

Ignition switches on the dashboard.

Trouser leg clips for bicycles without chain guards.

Soldering irons you heated on a gas burner.

Using hand signals for cars without turn indicators.

Older Than Dirt Quiz:

Count all the ones that you remember, not the ones you were told about.

Ratings at the bottom.

1. Sweet cigarettes
2. Coffee shops with juke boxes
3. Home milk delivery in glass bottles
4. Party lines on the telephone
5. Newsreels before the movie
6. TV test patterns that came on at night after the last show and were there until TV shows started again in the morning.. (There were only 2 channels)
7. Peashooters
8. 33 rpm records
9. 45 RPM records
10. Hi-fi's
11. Metal ice trays with levers
12. Blue flashbulb
13. Cork popguns
14. Wash tub wringers

If you remembered 0-3 = You're still young

If you remembered 3-6 = You are getting older

If you remembered 7-10 = Don't tell your age

If you remembered 11-14 = You're positively ancient!

Subject: 9 months later!!!

Jack decided to go skiing with his buddy, Bob. They loaded up Jack's minivan and headed north.

After driving for a few hours they got caught in a terrible blizzard. They pulled into a nearby farm and asked the attractive lady who answered the door if they could spend the night.

'I realize it's terrible weather out there and I have this huge house all to myself, but I'm recently widowed,' she explained. 'I'm afraid the neighbours will talk if I let you stay in my house.'

'Don't worry,' Jack said, 'we'll be happy to sleep in the barn, and if the weather breaks, we'll be gone at first light.' The lady agreed and the two men found their way to the barn and settled in for the night.

Come morning the weather had cleared and they got on their way. They enjoyed a great weekend of skiing.

About nine months later Jack got an unexpected letter from an attorney. It took him a few minutes to figure it out but he finally determined that it was from the attorney of that attractive widow he had met on the ski weekend.

He dropped in on his friend Bob and asked, 'Bob, do you remember that good-looking widow from the farm we stayed at on our ski holiday up north about 9 months ago?'

'Yes, I do.' Said Bob.

'Did you, er, happen to get up in the middle of the night, go up to the house and pay her a visit?'

'Well, um, yes!,' Bob said, a little embarrassed about being found out, 'I have to admit that I did.'

'And did you happen to give her my name instead of telling her your name?'

Bob's face turned beet red and he said,

'Yeah, look, I'm sorry, buddy. I'm afraid I did.' 'Why do you ask?'

'She just died and left me everything.'

Subject: At the Theatre

A man is lying, sprawled across 3 seats in the theatre.

The usher tried everything to make him use a single seat.

The usher went to get the manager.

In a few moments, both the usher and the manager returned and stood over the man. Together the two of them tried repeatedly to move him, but with no success. Finally, they summoned the police.

The cop surveyed the situation briefly then asked, "All right buddy, what's your name?"

"Sam," the man moaned. "Where ya from, Sam?"

With pain in his voice Sam replied "The balcony."

Subject: Brothel at the top of the Hill

There was a brothel at the top of a hill, with a large red light at the bottom of the hill.
There were four men ...
One was walking briskly up the hill;
one was inside the brothel;
one was walking slowly down the hill and
the fourth man was sitting in his car at the bottom of the hill.
What were the nationalities of the four men?
* The man going up the hill: was rushin
* The man in the brothel: him-a-layin
* The man walking down the hill: was finish
* The man in the car at the bottom was Irish.

He was waiting for the light to turn green.

The 'Perfect Password'

A woman was helping her husband set up his computer, and at the appropriate point in the process, the computer advised him that he would now need to enter a password. Something he will use to log on.
The husband was in a rather amorous mood and figured he would try for the shock effect to bring this to his wife's attention. So, when the computer asked him to enter his password, he made it plainly obvious to his wife what he was entering by stating each letter out loud as he typed:
P.....E.....N.....I.....S
His wife fell off her chair laughing when the computer replied:
**** PASSWORD REJECTED. NOT LONG ENOUGH****

Light travels faster than sound...
Which is why some people appear brilliant until you hear them.

There is a light at the end of every tunnel; just pray it's not a train coming

42.7 percent of all statistics are made up on the spot.

116

Subject: Little Bruce and Jenny are only 10 years old, but they know they are in love.

One day they decide that they want to get married, so Bruce goes to Jenny's father to ask him for her hand.

Bruce bravely walks up to him and says, "Mr. Smith, me and Jenny are in love and I want to ask you for her hand in marriage."

Thinking that this was just the cutest thing, Mr. Smith replies: "Well Bruce, you are only 10. Where will you two live?"

Without even taking a moment to think about it, Bruce replies: "In Jenny's room. It's bigger than mine and we can both fit there nicely."

Still thinking this is just adorable, Mr. Smith says with a huge grin: "Okay, then how will you live? You're not old enough to get a job. You'll need to support Jenny."

Again, Bruce instantly replies: "Our allowance, Jenny makes five bucks a week and I make 10 bucks a week. That's about 60 bucks a month, so that should do us just fine."

Mr. Smith is impressed as Bruce has put so much thought into this.

"Well Bruce, it seems like you have everything figured out. I just have one more question. What will you do if the two of you should have little children of your own?"

Bruce just shrugs his shoulders and says, "Well, we've been lucky so far."

Mr. Smith no longer thinks the little shit is adorable.

Subject: Dear Abby,

I have never written to you before, but I really need your advice. I have suspected for some time now that my wife has been cheating on me.

The usual signs; phone rings but if I answer, the caller hangs up. My wife has been going out with 'the girls' a lot recently although when I ask their names she always says, just some friends from work, you don't know them.

I stay awake and watch for her when she comes home, but I usually fall asleep.

Anyway, I have never broached the subject with my wife. I think deep down I just did not want to know the truth, but last night she went out again and I decided to finally check on her around midnight, I hid in the garage behind my golf clubs so I could get a good view of the whole street when she arrived home from a night out with "the girls."

When she got out of the car she was buttoning up her blouse, which was open, and she took her panties out of her purse and slipped them on.

It was at that moment, crouching behind my golf clubs, that I noticed a hairline crack where the grip meets the graphite shaft on my Taylor Made 460 driver.

Is this something I can fix myself or should I take it back to the PGA Superstore?

Signed...

Concerned Golfer

Subject: WHAT I WANT IN A MAN

What I Want In a Man, Original List
1. Handsome
2. Charming
3. Financially successful
4. A caring listener
5. Witty
6. In good shape
7. Dresses with style
8. Appreciates finer things
9. Full of thoughtful surprises

What I Want in a Man, Revised List (age 32)
1. Nice looking
2. Opens car doors, holds chairs
3. Has enough money for a nice dinner
4. Listens more than talks
5. Laughs at my jokes
6. Carries bags of groceries with ease
7. Owns at least one tie
8. Appreciates a good home-cooked meal
9. Remembers birthdays and anniversaries

What I Want in a Man, Revised List (age 42)
1. Not too ugly
2. Doesn't drive off until I'm in the car
3. Works steady - splurges on dinner out occasionally
4. Nods head when I'm talking
5. Usually remembers punch lines of jokes
6. Is in good enough shape to rearrange the furniture
7. Wears a shirt that covers his stomach
8. Knows not to buy champagne with screw-top lids
9. Remembers to put the toilet seat down
10. Shaves most weekends

What I Want in a Man, Revised List (age 52)
1. Keeps hair in nose and ears trimmed
2. Doesn't belch or scratch in public

3. Doesn't borrow money too often
4. Doesn't nod off to sleep when I'm venting
5. Doesn't re-tell the same joke too many times
6. Is in good enough shape to get off the couch on weekends
7. Usually wears matching socks and fresh underwear
8. Appreciates a good TV dinner
9. Remembers your name on occasion
10. Shaves some weekends

What I Want in a Man, Revised List (age 62)
1. Doesn't scare small children
2. Remembers where bathroom is
3. Doesn't require much money for upkeep
4. Only snores lightly when asleep
5.. Remembers why he's laughing
6. Is in good enough shape to stand up by himself
7. Usually wears some clothes
8. Likes soft foods
9. Remembers where he left his teeth
10. Remembers that it's the weekend

What I Want in a Man, Revised List (age 72)
1. Breathing.
2. Doesn't miss the toilet.

Subject: Married too long
After being married for 44 years, I took a careful look at my wife one day and said, "Darling, 44 years ago we had a cheap apartment, a cheap car, slept on a sofa bed and watched a 10-inch black and white TV, but I got to sleep every night with a hot 25-year-old girl. Now I have a $500,000 home, a $45,000 car, nice big bed and plasma screen TV, but I'm sleeping with a 65-year-old woman. It seems to me that you're not holding up your side of things."
My wife is a very reasonable woman. She told me to go out and find a hot 25-year-old gal, and she would make sure that I would once again be living in a cheap apartment, driving a cheap car, sleeping on a sofa bed and watching a 10-inch black and white TV.
Aren't older women great? They really know how to solve your mid-life crisis.

Subject: The scene is Bishoploch Primary School[13]

Glasgow teacher: 'Good morning children, today is Thursday, so we're going to have a general knowledge quiz.

The pupil who gets the answer right can have Friday and Monday off and not come back to school until Tuesday.'

Wee Murray thinks, 'Ya beauty! I'm dead brilliant at general knowledge, so I am. This is goannae be a doddle!'

Teacher: ' Right class, who can tell me who said. 'Don't ask what our country can do for you, but what you can do for your country?'

Wee Murray shoots up his hand, waving furiously in the air.

Teacher looking round picks Farquhar Fauntleroy at the front.

'Yes, Farquhar?' Farquhar (in a very English accent): ' Yes miss, the answer is J F Kennedy - inauguration speech 1960.'

Teacher: 'Very good Farquhar. You may stay off Friday and Monday and we will see you back in class on Tuesday.'

The next Thursday comes around, and Wee Murray is even more determined.

Teacher: 'Who said 'We will fight them on the beaches, we will fight them in the air, we will fight them at sea. But we will never surrender?' Wee Murray's hand shoots up, arm stiff as a board, shouting 'I know, I know. Pick me Miss, pick me Miss'.

Teacher looking round and picks Tarquin Smythe, sitting at the front: 'Yes Tarquin.'

Tarquin (in a very, very posh English accent): 'Yes miss, the answer is Winston Churchill, 1941 Battle of Britain speech.'

Teacher: 'Very good Tarquin, you may stay off Friday and Monday and come back to class on Tuesday.'

The following Thursday comes around and Wee Murray is hyper; he's been studying encyclopaedias all week and he's ready for anything that comes...

He's coiled in his chair, dribbling in anticipation.

Teacher: 'Who said 'One small step for man, one giant leap for mankind?'

Wee Murray's arm shoots straight in the air, he's standing on his seat, jumping up and down screaming 'Pick me miss. Pick me miss. I know, I know. Me Miss, me miss, meeeeee'.

Teacher looking round the class picks Rupert, sitting at the front.

'Yes, Rupert?' Rupert (in a frightfully, ever so plumy English accent):

'Miss that was Neil Armstrong, 1969, the first moon landing.'

Teacher: 'Very good Rupert. You may stay off Friday and Monday and come back into class on Tuesday.'

Wee Murray loses the plot altogether, tips his desk and throws his chair at the wall. He starts screaming: 'WHERE THE F**K DID ALL THESE ENGLISH B*ST*RDS COME FROM?'

Teacher spins back round from the blackboard and shouts: 'Who said that?'

Wee Murray grabs his coat and bag and heads for the door, 'Robert the Bruce, Bannockburn, 1314.

See ye on Tuesday Miss!

Subject: NO PLANTING TODAY

Two Irishmen were working for the city public works department. One would dig a hole and the other would follow behind him and fill the hole in. They worked up one side of the street, then down the other, then moved on to the next street, working furiously all day without rest, one man digging a hole, the other filling it in. An onlooker was amazed at their hard work, but couldn't understand what they were doing. So he asked the hole digger, 'I'm impressed by the effort you two are putting in to your work, but I don't get it – why do you dig a hole, only to have your partner follow behind and fill it up again?'

The hole digger wiped his brow and sighed, 'Well, I suppose it probably looks odd because we're normally a three-person team. But today the lad who plants the trees called in sick.'

Subject: The wedding night

A middle aged man and woman fall in love, and decide to get married. On their wedding night they settle into the bridal suite and the bride says to her new groom, "Please be gentle... I am still a virgin." The startled groom says "How can that be? You've been married twice..."

The bride responds... "Well you see it was this way: My first husband, he was a psychiatrist, and all he ever wanted to do was talk about sex.

Catching her breath, she says "My second husband was a stamp collector, and all he ever wanted to do ....was.............well.........

Oh God, I miss him so much!!!!"

A man is seriously ill in hospital. When he came to his senses, he motioned for his wife to come near. "You have been with me through all the bad times," he said. "When I got fired, you were there. When my business failed, you were there. When I got shot, you stayed by my side. When we lost the house, you gave me support. When my health started failing, you were still by my side. You know what?"

"What dear?" she asked gently.

"I think you bring me bad luck."

I've been in love with the same woman for forty-one years. If my wife finds out, she'll kill me.

Henry Youngman

Grandma used to set her hot baked apple pies on the window sill to cool
Her granddaughters set theirs on the window sill to thaw.

Subject: The Shipwreck

A man was washed up on a beach after a terrible shipwreck. Only a sheep and a sheepdog were washed up with him. After looking around, he realized that they were stranded on a deserted island.

After being there awhile, he got into the habit of taking his two animal companions to the beach every evening to watch the sunset. One particular evening, the sky was a fiery red with beautiful cirrus clouds, the breeze was warm and gentle - a perfect night for romance. As they sat there. the sheep started looking better and better to the lonely man. Soon, he leaned over to the sheep and put his arm around it. But the sheepdog, ever protective of the sheep, growled fiercely until the man took his arm from around the sheep.

After that, the three of them continued to enjoy the sunsets together, but there was no more cuddling.

A few weeks passed and behold, there was another shipwreck.

The only survivor was Cherie Blair[14].

That evening, the man brought Cherie to the evening beach ritual. It was another beautiful evening, red sky, cirrus clouds, a warm and gentle breeze - perfect for a night of romance. Pretty soon, the man started to get "those feelings" again.... He fought the urges as long as he could but he finally gave in and leaned over to Cherie and told her he hadn't had sex for months. Cherie battered her eyelashes and asked if there was anything she could do for him.

He said, "Would you mind taking the dog for a walk"

Subject: FW: Fwd: Daddy's Little Girl]

A father watched his young daughter playing in the garden.
He smiled as he reflected on how sweet and pure his little girl was.
Tears formed in his eyes as he thought about her seeing the wonders of nature through such innocent eyes.
Suddenly she just stopped and stared at the ground.
He went over to her to see what work of God had captured her attention.
He noticed she was looking at two spiders mating.
'Daddy, what are those two spiders doing?' she asked.
'They're mating,' her father replied.
'What do you call the spider on top?' she asked.
'That's a Daddy Longlegs,' her father answered.
'So, the other one is a Mommy Longlegs?' the little girl asked.
As his heart soared with the joy of such a cute and innocent question he replied, 'No dear. Both of them are Daddy Longlegs.'
'The little girl, looking a little puzzled, thought for a moment, then lifted her foot and stomped them flat.
'Well, we're not having any of that gay shit in our garden,' she said.

You burn more calories sleeping than you do watching television.

Subject: VATICAN HUMOR

After getting Pope Benedict's entire luggage loaded into the limo, (and he doesn't travel light), the driver notices the Pope is still standing on the curb.

'Excuse me, Your Holiness,' says the driver, 'Would you please take your seat so we can leave?'

'Well, to tell you the truth,' says the Pope, 'they never let me drive at the Vatican when I was a cardinal, and I'd really like to drive today.'

'I'm sorry, Your Holiness, but I cannot let you do that. I'd lose my job! What if something should happen?' protests the driver, wishing he'd never gone to work that morning.

'Who's going to tell?' says the Pope with a smile.

Reluctantly, the driver gets in the back as the Pope climbs in behind the wheel. The driver quickly regrets his decision when, after exiting the airport, the Pontiff floors it, accelerating the limo to 205 kph.. (Remember, the Pope is German.)

'Please slow down, Your Holiness!' pleads the worried driver, but the Pope keeps the pedal to the metal until they hear sirens.

'Oh, dear God, I'm going to lose my license -- and my job!' moans the driver.

The Pope pulls over and rolls down the window as the cop approaches, but the cop takes one look at him, goes back to his motorcycle, and gets on the radio.

'I need to talk to the Chief,' he says to the dispatcher.

The Chief gets on the radio and the cop tells him that he's stopped a limo going 205 kph.

'So bust him,' says the Chief.

'I don't think we want to do that, he's really important,' said the cop.

The Chief exclaimed,' All the more reason!'

'No, I mean really important,' said the cop with a bit of persistence.

The Chief then asked, 'Who do you have there, the mayor?'

Cop: 'Bigger.'

Chief: ' A senator?'

Cop: 'Bigger.'

Chief: 'The Prime Minister?'

Cop: 'Bigger.'

'Well,' said the Chief, 'who is it?'

Cop: 'I think it's God!'

The Chief is even more puzzled and curious, 'What makes you think it's God?'

Cop: 'His chauffeur is the Pope!'

One night two blondes sitting on a bench talking

One says to the other, "Which do you think is farther away, Florida or the moon"

The other blonde turns and says "Hellooooooooooo, can you SEE Florida...?????"

Subject: SCHOOL -- 1970 vs. TODAY

Scenario: Johnny and Mark get into a fistfight after school.

1970 - Crowd gathers. Johnny wins. Johnny and Mark shake hands and end up best mates for life.

TODAY - Police called, arrests Johnny and Mark. Charge them with assault, both expelled even though Mark started it. Both children go to anger management programs for 3 months. School board hold meeting to implement bullying prevention programs

Scenario: Robbie won't keep still in class, disrupts other students.

1970 – Robbie sent to office and given 6 of the best by the Headmaster. Returns to class, sits still and does not disrupt class again.

TODAY - Robbie given huge doses of Ritalin. Becomes a zombie. Tested for ADD. Robbie's parents get fortnightly disability payments and School gets extra funding from state because Robbie has a disability.

Scenario: Billy breaks a window in his neighbour's car and his Dad gives him a whipping with a belt.

1970 - Billy is more careful next time, grows up normal, goes to college, and becomes a successful businessman.

TODAY - Billy's dad is arrested for child abuse. Billy removed to foster care and joins a gang. Billy's sister tells Government psychologist that she remembers being abused herself and their dad goes to prison.

Scenario : Mark gets a headache and takes some aspirin to school.

1970 - Mark gets glass of water from Teacher to take aspirin with.

TODAY - Police called, Mark expelled from school for drug violations. Car searched for drugs and weapons.

Scenario: Johnny takes part leftover firecrackers from Guy Fawkes, puts them in a model air fix paint bottle, and blows up an ants nest.

1970 - Ants die.

TODAY- Police, Armed Forces, & Anti-terrorism Squad called. Johnny charged with domestic terrorism, MI5 investigate parents, siblings removed from home, computers confiscated. Johnny's dad goes on a terror watch list and is never allowed to fly again.

Scenario :

Johnny falls while running during break and scrapes his knee. He is found crying by his teacher, Mary . Mary hugs him to comfort him.

1970 - In a short time, Johnny feels better and goes on playing.

TODAY - Mary is accused of being a sexual predator and loses her job. She faces 3 years in Prison. Johnny undergoes 5 years of therapy.

Did you hear about the Pre-School teacher who was helping one of the children put on his "Wellie boots"?

He asked for help and she could see why. Even with her pulling and him pushing, the little "Wellies" still didn't want to go on. By the time they got the second "Wellie" on, she had worked up a sweat.

She almost cried when the little boy said, "Miss, they're on the wrong feet." She looked, and sure enough, they were. It wasn't any easier pulling the "Wellies" off than it was putting them on.

She managed to keep her cool as together they worked to get the "Wellies" back this time on the right feet.

He then announced, "These aren't my Wellies." She bit her tongue rather than get right in his face and scream, 'Why didn't you say so?' like she wanted to.

Once again, she struggled to help him pull the ill-fitting "Wellie's" off his little feet. No sooner had they gotten the "Wellie's" off when he said, "They're my brother's "Wellies", my mom made me wear them".

Now she didn't know if she should laugh or cry. But, she mustered up what grace and courage she had left to wrestle the "Wellies" on his feet again.

Helping him into his coat, she asked, "Now, where are your gloves?"

He said, "I stuffed 'them in the toes of my Wellies".

She will be eligible for parole in three years!

My parents recently retired. Mom always wanted to learn to play the piano, so dad bought her a piano for her birthday. A few weeks later, I asked how she was doing with it. "Oh, we returned the piano." said My Dad, "I persuaded her to switch to a clarinet instead." "How come?" I asked. "Because," he answered, "with a clarinet, she can't sing."

Quantum Mechanics: The dreams stuff is made of.

I just brought a friend of mine a new fridge. Should have seen his face light up when he opened it

Subject: Silly Joke

You promised me to send an electrician to fix the door bell, three days have gone by, and nobody has come.

I did send a guy. But he pushed the bell, nobody opened the door.

Subject: Things that are **difficult** to say when drunk:

1. Innovative
2. Preliminary
3. Proliferation
4. Cinnamon

Things that are **very difficult** to say when drunk:

1. Specificity
2. Anti-constitutionalistically
3. Passive-aggressive disorder
4. Transubstantiate

Things that are **downright impossible** to say when drunk:

1. No thanks, I'm married.
2. Nope, no more booze for me!
3. Sorry, but you're not really my type.
4. Kebab ? No thanks, I'm not hungry.
5. Good evening, officer. Isn't it lovely out tonight?
6. Oh, I couldn't! No one wants to hear me sing karaoke.
7. I'm not interested in fighting you.
8. Thank you, but I won't make any attempt to dance, I have no coordination. I'd hate to look like a fool!
9. Where is the nearest bathroom? I refuse to pee in this parking lot or on the side of the road.
10. I must be going home now, as I have to work in the morning

This blonde went to the pizza place and ordered a pizza. The pizza guy asked her if she wanted it cut into six pieces or twelve.
"Oh, six," she said. "I could never eat twelve pieces."

Subject: Outside a London second-hand shop:

We exchange anything - bicycles, washing machines, etc.
Why not bring your wife along and get a wonderful bargain?

126

Subject: FIFTY BUCKS IS FIFTY BUCKS

Ken and his wife Edna went to the state fair every year,

And every year Ken would say,

'Edna, I'd like to ride in that helicopter

Edna always replied,

'I know Ken, but that helicopter ride is fifty bucks,

And fifty bucks is fifty bucks'

One year Ken and Edna went to the fair, and Ken said,

'Edna, I'm 75 years old.

If I don't ride that helicopter, I might never get another chance'

To this, Edna replied,

"Ken that helicopter ride is fifty bucks, and fifty bucks is fifty bucks'

The pilot overheard the couple and said,

'Folks I'll make you a deal. I'll take the both of you for a ride. If you can stay

quiet for the entire ride and don't say a word I won't charge you a penny!

But if you say one word its fifty dollars.'

Ken and Edna agreed and up they went.

The pilot did all kinds of fancy manoeuvres, but not a word was heard.

He did his daredevil tricks over and over again, but still not a word...

When they landed, the pilot turned to Ken and said,

'By golly, I did everything I could to get you to yell out, but you didn't.

I'm impressed!' Ken replied,

'Well, to tell you the truth, I almost said something when Edna fell out,

But you know,

"Fifty bucks is fifty bucks!'

A bartender is just a pharmacist with a limited inventory.   *-Albert Einstein*

The hardest thing in life is to do nothing...
You never know when you're finished.

This is a genuine complaint to Greenock[15] Police Force from an angry member of the public. A true email sent to the force.

Dear Sir/Madam/Automated telephone answering service,

Having spent the past twenty minutes waiting for someone at Greenock police station to pick up a telephone I have decided to abandon the idea and try e-mailing you instead.

Perhaps you would be so kind as to pass this message on to your colleagues in Greenock , by means of smoke signal, carrier pigeon or Ouija board.

As I'm writing this e-mail there are eleven failed medical experiments (I think you call them youths) in Mathie Crescent, which is just off Mathie Road in Gourock.

Six of them seem happy enough to play a game which involves kicking a football against an iron gate with the force of a meteorite. This causes an earth shattering CLANG! which rings throughout the entire building. This game is now in its third week and as I am unsure how the scoring system works, I have no idea if it will end any time soon.

The remaining five failed-abortions are happily rummaging through several bags of rubbish and items of furniture that someone has so thoughtfully dumped beside the wheelie bins.

One of them has found a saw and is setting about a discarded chair like a beaver on ecstasy pills.

I fear that it's only a matter of time before they turn their limited attention to the caravan gas bottle that is lying on its side between the two bins. If they could be relied on to only blow their own arms and legs off then I would happily leave them to it. I would even go so far as to lend them the matches. Unfortunately they are far more likely to blow up half the street with them and I've just finished decorating the kitchen.

What I suggest is this - after replying to this e-mail with worthless assurances that the matter is being looked into and will be dealt with, why not leave it until the one night of the year (probably bath night) when there are no mutants around then drive up the street in a Panda car before doing a three point turn and disappearing again. This will of course serve no other purpose than to remind us what policemen actually look like. I trust that when I take a claw hammer to the skull of one of these throwbacks you'll do me the same courtesy of giving me a four month head start before coming to arrest me.

I remain your obedient servant

Reply

Mr X, I have read your e-mail and understand your frustration at the problems caused by youths playing in the area and the problems you have encountered in trying to contact the police.

As the Community Beat Officer for your street I would like to extend an offer of discussing the matter fully with you. Should you wish to discuss the matter, please provide contact details (address / telephone number) and when may be suitable.

Regards PC Plod, Community Beat Officer

Reply
Dear PC Plod
First of all I would like to thank you for the speedy response to my original e-mail. 16 hours and 38 minutes must be a personal record for Greenock Police Station, and rest assured that I will forward these details to Norris McWhirter for inclusion in his next Guinness Book of Records.
Secondly I was delighted to hear that our street has its own Community Beat Officer.
May I be the first to congratulate you on your covert skills? In the five or so years I have lived in Mathie Crescent , I have never seen you. Do you hide up a tree or have you gone deep undercover and infiltrated the gang itself? Are you the one with the acne and the moustache on his forehead or the one with a chin like a wash hand basin? It's surely only a matter of time before you are head-hunted by MI5.
Whilst I realise that there may be far more serious crimes taking place in Gourock, such as smoking in a public place or being a Christian without due care and attention, is it too much to ask for a policeman to explain (using words of no more than two syllables at a time) to these twats that they might want to play their strange football game elsewhere?
The pitch on Larkfield Road or the one at Battery Park are both within spitting distance, as is the bottom of the Gourock Dock, the latter being the preferred option especially if the tide is in.
Should you wish to discuss these matters further you should feel free to contact me on xxxxxxxx. If after 25 minutes I have still failed to answer, I'll buy you a large one in Monty's Pub.
Regards X
P.S If you think that this is sarcasm, think yourself lucky that you don't work for the sewerage department with whom I am also in contact!!!

Q. Whats the difference between a wife and a girlfriend ?
A. 50 pounds

Subject: Half The Job
"This little computer," said the salesman, "will do half of your job for you."
Studying the machine, the senior VP said, "Fine, I'll take two."

> *Going to Starbucks for coffee is like going to prison for sex.*
> *You know you're going to get it, but it's going to be rough.*

Subject: In this life I'm a woman.

In my next life, I'd like to come back as a bear. When you're a bear, you get to hibernate. You do nothing but sleep for six months.
I could deal with that.
Before you hibernate, you're supposed to eat yourself stupid. I could deal with that, too.
When you're a girl bear, you birth your children (who are the size of walnuts) while you're sleeping and wake up to partially grown, cute cuddly cubs. I could definitely deal with that.
If you're a mama bear, everyone knows you mean business. You swat anyone who bothers your cubs. If your cubs get out of line, you swat them too. I could deal with that. If you're a bear, your mate EXPECTS you to wake up growling. He EXPECTS that you will have hairy legs and excess body fat.
Yup... gonna be a bear.

Subject: Fwd: The knob

A woman in her forties went to a plastic surgeon for a face-lift. The surgeon told her about a new procedure called "The Knob," where a small knob is placed on the back of a woman's head and can be turned to tighten up her skin to produce the effect of a brand new face lift.
Of course, the woman wanted "The Knob."
Over the course of the years, the woman tightened the knob, and the effects were wonderful -- the woman remained young looking and vibrant.
After fifteen years, the woman returned to the surgeon with two problems.
"All these years, everything has been working just fine. I've had to turn the knob and I've always loved the results. But now I've developed two annoying problems:
First, I have these terrible bags under my eyes and the knob won't get rid of them."
The doctor looked at her closely and said, "Those aren't bags, those are your tits."
She said, "No point asking about the beard then............"

When I was young I used to pray for a bike, then I realized that God doesn't work that way, so I stole a bike and prayed for forgiveness.

Subject: What starts with F and ends with K?

A first-grade teacher, Ms Brooks, was having trouble with one of her students. The teacher asked, *'Harry, what's your problem?'*

Harry answered, *'I'm too smart for the 1st grade. My sister is in the 3rd grade and I'm smarter than she is! I think I should be in the 3rd grade too!'*

Ms. Brooks had had enough. She took Harry to the principal's office.

While Harry waited in the outer office, the teacher explained to the principal what the situation was. The principal told Ms. Brooks he would give the boy a test. If he failed to answer any of his questions he was to go back to the 1st grade and behave. She agreed.

Harry was brought in and the conditions were explained to him and he agreed to take the test.

Principal:
'What is 3 x 3?'   Harry: *'9.'*

Principal:
'What is 6 x 6?'   Harry: *'36.'*

And so it went with every question the principal thought a 3rd grader should know. The principal looks at Ms. Brooks and tells her, *'Harry can go to the 3rd grade'*

Ms. Brooks says to the principal, *'Let me ask him some more questions.'*

The principal and Harry both agreed.

Ms. Brooks asks, *'What does a cow have four of, that I have only two of?'*

Harry, after a moment: *'Legs.'*

Ms. Brooks: *'What is in your pants that you have but I do not have?'*

The principal wondered why would she ask such a question!

Harry replied: *'Pockets.'*

Ms. Brooks: *'What does a dog do that a man steps into?'*

Harry: *'Pants.'*

The principal sat forward with his mouth hanging open.

Ms. Brooks: *'What goes in hard and pink then comes out soft and sticky?'*

The principal's eyes opened really wide and before he could stop the answer, Harry replied, 'Bubble gum.'

Ms. Brooks: 'What does a man do standing up, a woman does sitting down and a dog does on three legs?' Harry: 'Shake hands .'

The principal was trembling.

Ms. Brooks: 'What word starts with an 'F' and ends in 'K' that means a lot of heat and excitement?'

Harry: 'Firetruck.'

The principal breathed a sigh of relief and told the teacher,

'Put Harry in the fifth-grade, I got the last seven questions wrong.

*The first half of our life is ruined by our parents and the second half by our children.   **Clarence Darrow***

Subject: From The London Times: A Well-Planned Retirement

A perfect example of government mismanagement.

Outside England 's Bristol Zoo there is a parking lot for 150 cars and 8 buses. For 25 years, its parking fees were managed by a very pleasant attendant. The fees were for cars (£1.40), for buses (about £7).

Then, one day, after 25 solid years of never missing a day of work, he just didn't show up; so the Zoo Management called the City Council and asked it to send them another parking agent.

The Council did some research and replied that the parking lot was the Zoo's own responsibility.

The Zoo advised the Council that the attendant was a City employee.

The City Council responded that the lot attendant had never been on the City payroll.

Meanwhile, sitting in his villa somewhere on the coast of Spain or France or Italy ... there is a man who'd apparently had a ticket machine installed completely on his own and then had simply begun to show up every day, commencing to collect and keep the parking fees, estimated at about £560 per day -- for 25 years.

Assuming 7 days a week, this amounts to just over 7 million pounds ... and no one even knows his name.

Subject: FW: CLASSIC Wisdom from the Farm...

A little boy comes down to breakfast. Since they live on farm, his mother asks if he had done his chores. "Not yet," said the little boy.

His mother tells him no breakfast until he does his chores.

Well, he's a little ticked off, so he goes to feed the chickens, and he kicks a chicken. He goes to feed the cows, and he kicks a cow. He goes to feed the pigs, and he kicks a pig. He goes back in for breakfast and his mother gives him a bowl of dry cereal.

"How come I don't get any eggs and bacon? Why don't I have any milk in my cereal?" he asks.

"Well," his mother says, "I saw you kick a chicken, so you don't get any eggs for a week. I saw you kick the pig, so you don't get any bacon for a week. I saw you kick the cow so for a week you aren't getting any milk."

Just then, his father comes down for breakfast and kicks the cat halfway across the kitchen.

The little boy looks up at his mother with a smile, and says,
"Are you gonna tell him, or should I ??

Subject: A DAMN FINE EXPLANATION

The wife came home early and found her husband in their bedroom making love to a very attractive young woman.

And she was somewhat upset. 'You are a disrespectful pig!' she cried.

'How dare you do this to me -- a faithful wife, the mother of your children? I want a divorce right away!'

And the husband replied, 'Hang on just a minute so at least I can tell you what happened.

'Fine, go ahead,' she sobbed,' but they'll be the last words you'll say to me!'

And the husband began –

'Well, I left work and was getting into the car to drive home, and this young lady here asked me for a lift. She looked so down and out and defenceless that I took pity on her and let her into the car.

I noticed that she was very thin, not well dressed and very dirty. She told me that she hadn't eaten for three days. So, in my compassion, I brought her home and warmed up the enchiladas I made for you last night, the ones you wouldn't eat because you're afraid you'll put on weight. The poor thing devoured them in moments.

Since she needed a good clean-up, I suggested a shower, and while she was doing that, I noticed her clothes were dirty and full of holes, so I threw them away.

Then, as she needed clothes, I gave her the designer jeans that you have had for a few years, but don't wear because you say they are too tight.

I also gave her the underwear that was your anniversary present, which you don't wear because I don't have good taste.

I found the sexy blouse my sister gave you for Christmas that you don't wear just to annoy her, and I also donated those boots you bought at the expensive boutique and don't wear because someone at work has a pair the same.'

The husband took a quick breath and continued - 'She was so grateful for my understanding and help that as I walked her to the door, she turned to me with tears in her eyes and said, 'Please ... Do you have anything else that your wife doesn't use?'

So, since you haven't been using it !!!!!!!!!!...............

My husband and I divorced over religious differences.
He thought he was God and I didn't

133

Subject: The Pharmacist and the Wife

Upon arriving home, a husband was met at the door by his sobbing wife. Tearfully, she explained, "It's the pharmacist. He insulted me terribly This morning on the phone. I had to call multiple times before he would even answer the phone." Immediately, the husband drove downtown to confront the pharmacist and demand an apology.

Before he could say more than a word or two, the pharmacist told him, "Now, just a minute, listen to my side of it. This morning, the alarm failed to go off, so I was late getting up. I went without breakfast and hurried out to the car, just to realize that I'd locked the house with both house and car keys inside and had to break a window to get my keys.

"Then, driving a little too fast, I got a speeding ticket. Later, when I was about three blocks from the store, I had a flat tire."

"When I finally got to the store, a bunch of people were waiting for me to open up. I got the store opened and started waiting on these people. All the time, the darn phone was ringing off the hook." He continued, "Then, I had to break a roll of nickels against the cash register drawer to make change, and they spilled all over the floor. I had to get down on my hands and knees to pick up the nickels, and the phone was still ringing. When I came up cracked my head on the open cash drawer, which made me stagger back against a showcase with a bunch of perfume bottles on it. Half of them hit the floor and broke."

"Meanwhile, the phone is still ringing and I finally got back to answer it. It was your wife. She wanted to know how to use a rectal thermometer. **And believe me mister, as God is my witness, all I did was tell her.**"

Subject: 11 PEOPLE ON A ROPE

Eleven people were hanging on a rope under a helicopter.

10 men and 1 woman.

The rope was not strong enough to carry them all so they decided that one had to leave, because otherwise they were all going to fall to a certain death.

They weren't able to choose that person, until the woman gave a very touching speech.

She said that she would voluntarily let go of the rope, because, as a woman, she was used to giving up everything for her husband and kids or for men in general, and was used to always making sacrifices with little in return.

As soon as she finished her speech,

All the men started clapping.....

Never mess with women.

What if there were no hypothetical questions?

Subject: SIPPING VODKA

A new Priest at his first mass was so nervous he could hardly speak.
After mass he asked the Monsignor how he had done.
The Monsignor replied, *"When I am worried about getting nervous in the pulpit, I put a glass of vodka next to the water glass. If I start to get nervous, I take a sip..."*
So next Sunday he took the Monsignor's advice. At the beginning of the sermon, he got nervous and took a drink. He proceeded to talk up a storm.
Upon his return to his office after the mass, he found the following note on the door:
1) Sip the vodka, don't gulp.
2) There are 10 commandments, not 12.
3) There are 12 disciples, not 10.
4) Jesus was consecrated, not constipated.
5) Jacob wagered his donkey, he did not bet his ass.
6) We do not refer to Jesus Christ as the late J.C.
7) The Father, Son, and Holy Ghost are not referred to as Daddy, Junior and the Spook.
8) David slew Goliath; he did not kick the shit out of him.
9) When David was hit by a rock and was knocked off his donkey, don't say he was stoned off his ass.
10) We do not refer to the cross as the 'Big T.'
11) When Jesus broke the bread at the last supper he said, *"Take this and eat it for this is my body."* He did not say, *"Eat me."*
12) The Virgin Mary is not called 'Mary without the Cherry'.
13) The recommended grace before a meal is not: Rub-A-Dub-Dub thanks for the grub, Yeah God.
14) Next Sunday there will be a taffy pulling contest at St. Peter's not a Peter pulling contest at St. Taffy's.

Shakespeare walks into a tavern.
The barman says "You can't come in here, you're Bard"

Subject: Girls night out

Two women friends had gone out for a Girls Night Out, and had been decidedly over-enthusiastic on the cocktails. Incredibly drunk and walking home they suddenly realized they both needed to pee. They were very near a graveyard and one of them suggested they do their business behind a headstone or something. The first woman had nothing to wipe with so she took off her panties, used them and threw them away. Her friend however was wearing an expensive underwear set and didn't want to ruin hers, but was lucky enough to salvage a large ribbon from a wreath that was on a grave and proceeded to wipe herself with it. After finishing, they made their way home.

The next day the first woman's husband phones the other husband and said, "These damn girls' nights out have got to stop. My wife came home last night without her panties." "That's nothing," said the other. "Mine came back with a sympathy card stuck between the cheeks of her butt that said, **'From all of us at the Fire Station, We'll never forget you!'**

Subject: Feel Better

Mary was having a tough day and stretched herself out on the couch to do a bit of what she thought to be well-deserved complaining and self- pitying. She moaned to her mom and brother, "Nobody loves me, the whole world hates me!"

Her brother, busily occupied playing a computer game, hardly looked up at her and passed on this encouraging word:

"That's not true, Mary. Some people don't even know you."

Subject: Speech Impediment

Two life-long friends were enjoying a few pints down at the local bar, when one said to the other:

"If I ask you a question, will you promise to answer me honestly?"

"Yeah, sure thing," replied his friend, "fire away."

"Well," said the first guy, "why do you think all the guys around here find my wife so attractive?"

"It's probably because of her speech impediment," replied the second guy.

"What do you mean her speech impediment?" inquired the first fellow.

"My wife doesn't have a speech impediment!"

"Well," replied his friend, "you must be the only guy who hasn't noticed that she can't say 'NO'!"

Subject: Fwd: Ten dollar bills!!!

A man walks into a bar, notices a very large jar on the counter, and sees that it's filled to the brim with $10 bills. He guesses there must be at least ten thousand dollars in it. He approaches the bartender and asks, "What's with the money in the jar?"

"Well..., you pay $10, and if you pass three tests, you get all the money in the jar."
The man certainly isn't going to pass this up, so he asks,
"What are the three tests?"

"You gatta pay first," says the bartender, "those are the rules."
So, after thinking it over a while, the man gives the bartender $10 which he stuffs into the jar.

"Okay," says the bartender, "here's what you need to do:
First - You have to drink a whole quart of tequila, in 60 seconds or less, and you can't make a face while doing it."

"Second - There's a pit bull chained in the back with a bad tooth. You have to remove that tooth with your bare hands."

"Third - There's a 90-year old lady upstairs who's never had sex. You have to take care of that problem."

The man is stunned! "I know I paid my $10 - but I'm not an idiot! I won't do it! You'd have to be nuts to drink a quart of tequila and then do all those other things!"

"Your call," says the bartender, "but, your money stays where it is."
As time goes on, the man has a few more drinks and finally says, "Where's the damn tequila?!"

He grabs the bottle with both hands and drinks it as fast as he can.
Tears stream down both cheeks - but he doesn't make a face - and he drinks it in 58 seconds!

Next, he staggers out the back door where he sees the pit bull chained to a pole.
Soon, the people inside the bar hear loud growling, screaming, and sounds of a terrible fight - then nothing but silence!

Just when they think that the man surely must be dead, he staggers back into the bar. His clothes are ripped to shreds and he's bleeding from bites and gashes all over his body.

He drunkenly says, "Now..., where's that old woman with the bad tooth?"

A senior in college took his blonde girlfriend to a football game. As the game started, he said, "Watch the guy wearing number 15. I expect him to be our best man next year."

"Oh, Honey," she said. "That's such a clever way to propose. I accept!"

Subject: FW: An Irish Ghost Story

This story happened a while ago in Dublin, and even though it sounds like an Alfred Hitchcock tale, it's true.

John Bradford, a Dublin University student, was on the side of the road hitchhiking on a very dark night and in the midst of a storm. The night was rolling on and no car went by. The storm was so strong he could hardly see a few feet ahead of him.

Suddenly, he saw a car slowly coming towards him and stopped.

John, desperate for shelter and without thinking about it, got into the car and closed the door, only to realize there was nobody behind the wheel and the engine wasn't on. The car started moving slowly. John looked at the road ahead and saw a curve approaching. Scared, he started to pray, begging for his life. Then, just before the car hit the curve, a hand appeared out of nowhere through the window, and turned the wheel. John, paralyzed with terror, watched as the hand came through the window, but never touched or harmed him. Shortly thereafter, John saw the lights of a pub appear down the road, so, gathering strength; he jumped out of the car and ran to it. Wet and out of breath, he rushed inside and started telling everybody about the horrible experience he had just had.

A silence enveloped the pub when everybody realized he was crying, and wasn't drunk.

Suddenly, the door opened, and two other people walked in from the dark and stormy night. They, like John, were also soaked and out of breath.

Looking around, and seeing John Bradford sobbing at the bar, one said to the other.

Look Paddy, there's that fecking eejit that got in the car while we were pushing it!!'

Subject: Blonde GUY Joke

A blonde guy goes to a football game and finds his place in the bleachers. After a while, someone far behind him yells, "Hey, George."

The blonde gets up and scans the crowd behind him. Not seeing anyone he recognizes, he sits down.

Sometime later, someone yells again, "Hey, George."

The blonde gets up again and looks around. Seeing no one he knows, he sits down.

A third time someone yells, "Hey, George."

Finally, the blonde gets up, turns around and yells back,

"Knock it off! My name's not George."

These insults are from an era before the English language got boiled down to 4-letter words.

The exchange between **Churchill & Lady Astor**[16]:
She said, "If you were my husband I'd give you poison."
He said, "If you were my wife, I'd drink it."

A Member of Parliament to Disraeli[17]: "Sir, you will either die on the gallows or of some unspeakable disease." "That depends, Sir," said Disraeli, "whether I embrace your policies or your mistress."

"He had delusions of adequacy." - **Walter Kerr**[18]

"I have never killed a man, but I have read many obituaries with great pleasure." **Clarence Darrow**[19]

"He has never been known to use a word that might send a reader to the dictionary." - William Faulkner[20] **(about Ernest Hemingway).**

"Thank you for sending me a copy of your book; I'll waste no time reading it." -**Moses Hadas**[21]

"I didn't attend the funeral, but I sent a nice letter saying I approved of it." - Mark Twain

"He has no enemies, but is intensely disliked by his friends." - **Oscar Wilde**

**"I am enclosing two tickets to the first night of my new play; bring a friend.... if you have one." - George Bernard Shaw to Winston Churchill.
"Cannot possibly attend first night, will attend second.... if there is one." - Winston Churchill, in response.**

"He is a self-made man and worships his creator." - **John Bright**

"I feel so miserable without you; it's almost like having you here." - Stephen Bishop[22]

"He is not only dull himself; he is the cause of dullness in others."
- Samuel Johnson[23]

"I've just learned about his illness. Let's hope it's nothing trivial." - Irvin S. Cobb[24]

"In order to avoid being called a flirt, she always yielded easily." -
Charles, Count Talleyrand[25]

"He is simply a shiver looking for a spine to run up." - Paul Keating[26]

"He loves nature in spite of what it did to him.**" - Forrest Tucker**[27]

"His mother should have thrown him away and kept the stork." - Mae West

"Some cause happiness **wherever** they go; others, **whenever** they go." - **Oscar Wilde**

"He uses statistics as a drunken man uses lamp-posts. . for support rather than illumination. " - Andrew Lang (1844-1912)[28]

"He has Van Gogh's ear for music." **- Billy Wilder**[29]

"I've had a perfectly wonderful evening. But this wasn't it." - Groucho Marx

"Why do you sit there looking like an envelope without any address on it?" - **Mark Twain**

Subject: Secret Password

During her company's periodic password audit, a blond employee was found to be using this password:
GoofyHueyLouieDeweyDaisyDonaldMickeyMinnieWashington
When she was asked why she had such a long password, she said, "The boss said that my password had to be at least eight characters long and have at least one capital."

Subject: Mermaid or a whale?

Recently, in a large city in Australia, a poster featuring a young, thin and tan woman appeared in the window of a gym.

It said, "This summer, do you want to be a mermaid or a whale?"

A middle-aged woman, whose physical shape did not match those of the woman on the poster, responded to the question posed by the gym.

To Whom It May Concern,

Whales are always surrounded by friends (dolphins, sea lions, curious humans.) They have an active sex life, get pregnant and have adorable baby whales.

They have a wonderful time with dolphins stuffing themselves with shrimp.

They play and swim in the seas, seeing wonderful places like Patagonia, the Bering Sea and the coral reefs of Polynesia.

Whales are wonderful singers and have even recorded CDs.

They are incredible creatures and virtually have no predators other than humans. They are loved, protected and admired by almost everyone in the world.

Mermaids don't exist. If they did exist, they would be lining up outside the offices of psychoanalysts due to an identity crisis. Fish or human?

They don't have a sex life because they kill men who get close to them, not to mention how could they have sex?

Just look at them ... where is IT?

Therefore, they don't have kids either. How DO they reproduce?

Not to mention, who wants to get close to a girl who smells like fish?

The choice is perfectly clear to me: I want to be a whale.

P.S. We are in an age when media puts into our heads the idea that only skinny people are beautiful, but I prefer to enjoy an ice cream with my kids, a good dinner with a man who makes me shiver, and a piece of chocolate with my friends. With time, we gain weight because we accumulate so much information and wisdom in our heads that when there is no more room, it distributes out to the rest of our bodies.

So we aren't heavy, we are enormously cultured, educated and happy.

Beginning today, when I look at my butt in the mirror I will think.

Good grief, look how smart I am! ¨

What do you call a dog with no legs?
Nothing... he ain't gonna come, when you call him anyway

A prisoner of war is a man who tries to kill you and fails, and then asks you not to kill him. ~Sir Winston Churchill

141

Subject: Prostate check-up

A man goes to his doctor for his physical and gets sent to the Urologist as a precaution. When he gets there, he discovers the Urologist is a very pretty female doctor.

The female doctor says, "I'm going to check your prostate today, but this new procedure is a little different from what you are probably used to. I want you to lie on your right side, bend your knees, then while I check your prostate, take a deep breath and say, '99'.

The guy obeys and says,"99".

The doctor says, "Great". Now turn over on your left side and again, while repeat the check, take a deep breath and say, '99"..

Again, the guy says, '99'."

The doctor said, "Very good". Now then, I want you to lie on your back with your knees raised slightly. I'm going to check your prostate with this hand, and with the other hand I'm going to hold on to your penis to keep it out of the way.

Now take a deep breath and say, '99'.

The guy begins, "One ... Two ...Three".

Subject: Sunday School Class

I was testing children in my Glasgow Sunday School class to see if they understood the concept of getting into heaven.

I asked them, "If I sold my house and my Car, had a big jumble sale and gave all my Money to the church, would that get me into heaven?"

"NO!" the children answered.

"If I cleaned the church every day, mowed the garden and kept everything tidy, would that get me into heaven?"

Again, the answer was 'No!'

By now I was starting to smile.

"Well, then, if I was kind to animals and gave sweeties to all the children, and loved my husband, would that get me into heaven?"

Again, they all answered 'No!'

I was just bursting with pride for them.

I continued, "Then how can I get into heaven?"

A six year old boy shouted,

"Yuv got tae be fukin' deid[9]"

Kinda brings a wee tear tae yir eye....

Depression is merely anger without enthusiasm

American Airlines saved $40,000 in 1987 by eliminating one olive from each salad served in first-class.

Subject: Ever wonder why?

Why the sun lightens our hair, but darkens our skin?

Why women can't put on mascara, with their mouths closed?

Why we never see the headline 'Psychic wins lottery'?

Why is abbreviated such a long word?

Why is it that doctors call what they do 'PRACTICE'?

Why is lemon juice made with artificial flavour and dishwashing liquid made with real lemons?

Why is it that the man who invests all our money called a BROKER?

Why is the time of day with the slowest traffic, called RUSH HOUR?

Why don't sheep shrink when it rains?

Why are they called APARTMENTS when they are all stuck together?

If flying is so safe why do they call the airport the TERMINAL?

Why do supermarkets make sick people walk all the way to the back of the store to get their medical prescriptions, when healthy people can buy cigarettes at the front?

Why do people order DOUBLE CHEESEBURGERS, LARGE FRIES **AND a DIET COKE?**

Why do we leave cars worth thousands of pounds on the driveway and put our useless junk in the garage?

Why do they have drive-up ATM's with Braille lettering?

Subject: Cannibal Food

Two cannibals meet one day. The first cannibal says, "You know, I just can't seem to get a tender missionary. I've baked 'em, I've roasted 'em, I've stewed 'em, I've barbequed 'em, I've even tried every sort of marinade. I just cannot seem to get them tender."

The second cannibal asks, "What kind of missionary do you use?"

The other replied, "You know, the ones that hang out at that place at the bend of the river. They have those brown cloaks with a rope around the waist and their sort of bald on top with a funny ring of hair on their heads."

"Ah ha!" he replies. "No wonder,. those are friars!"

The longest sentence known to man: "I do."

Subject: A lesson in life.....The Gunslinger

An old prospector shuffled into the town of El Indio, Texas leading an old tired mule. The old man headed straight for the only saloon in town, to clear his parched throat.

He walked up to the saloon and tied his old mule to the hitch rail. As he stood there, brushing some of the dust from his face and clothes, a young gunslinger stepped out of the saloon with a gun in one hand and a bottle of whiskey in the other.

The young gunslinger looked at the old man and laughed, saying, "Hey old man, have you ever danced?"

The old man looked up at the gunslinger and said, "No, I never did dance .... never really wanted to."

A crowd had gathered as the gunslinger grinned and said, "Well, you old fool, you're gonna dance now," and started shooting at the old man's feet.

The old prospector, not wanting to get a toe blown off, started hopping around like a flea on a hot skillet.

Everybody was laughing, fit to be tied.

When his last bullet had been fired, the young gunslinger, still laughing, holstered his gun and turned around to go back into the saloon.

The old man turned to his pack mule, pulled out a double-barrelled shotgun, and cocked both hammers. The loud clicks carried clearly through the desert air.

The crowd stopped laughing immediately. The young gunslinger heard the sounds too, and he turned around very slowly. The silence was almost deafening.

The crowd watched as the young gunman stared at the old timer and the large gaping holes of those twin 10 gauge barrels. The barrels of the shotgun never wavered in the old man's hands, as he quietly said, "Son, have you ever kissed a mule's ass?"

The gunslinger swallowed hard and said, "No sir ... but... I've always wanted to."

There are a few lessons for us all here:

*Never be arrogant.
*Don't waste ammunition.
*Whiskey makes you think you're smarter than you are.
*Always, always make sure you know who has the power.
*Don't mess with old folks; they didn't get old by being stupid.

Subject: All Seniors Aren't Senile

An elderly, white-haired man walked into a jewellery store one Friday evening with a beautiful young blonde at his side.

He told the jeweller he was looking for a special ring for his girlfriend.

The jeweller looked through his stock and brought out a £5,000 ring. The old man said, "No, I'd like to see something more special."

At that statement, the jeweller went to his special stock and brought another ring over. "Here's a stunning ring at only £40,000," he said.

The young lady's eyes sparkled and her whole body trembled with excitement. The old man seeing this said, "We'll take it."

The jeweller asked how payment would be made and the old man stated, "By cheque. I know you need to make sure my cheque clears so I'll write it now, and you can call the bank on Monday morning to verify the funds and I'll pick the ring up on Monday afternoon," he said.

On Monday morning, the jeweller 'phoned the old man and said "Sir, there's no money in that account."

"I know," said the old man, "but let me tell you about my weekend!

Jock and an Englishman were flying from Edinburgh when the stewardess approached. "May I get you something?" she asked. "Aye, a whusky" Jock replied.

She poured him a drink then asked the Englishman if he'd like one.

"Never!" he said sternly. "I'd rather be raped and ravished by whores all the way to America than drink whisky!"

Jock hurriedly passed the drink back, saying "Och, Ah didna ken there wuz a choice!"

A rabbi took a job at a Duracell factory. His job is to stand on the production line and as the batteries go by, say, "I wish you long life".

I've used up all my sick days, so I'm calling in dead.

Interesting Factoids, Very Interesting, things some you might not know!!

Alaska - More than half of the coastline of the entire United States is in Alaska.

Amazon - The Amazon rainforest produces more than 20% of the world's oxygen supply.

The Amazon River pushes so much water into the Atlantic Ocean that, more than one hundred miles at sea, off the mouth of the river; one can dip fresh water out of the ocean.

The volume of water in the Amazon river is greater than the next eight largest rivers in the world combined and three times the flow of all rivers in the United States.

Antarctica -is the only land on our planet that is not owned by any country.

Ninety percent of the world's ice covers Antarctica.

This ice also represents seventy percent of all the fresh water in the world.

As strange as it sounds, however, Antarctica is essentially a desert; The average yearly total precipitation is about two inches.

Antarctica is the driest place on the planet, with an absolute humidity lower than the Gobi desert.

Brazil - got its name from the nut, not the other way around.

Canada - has more lakes than the rest of the world combined.

Canada is an Indian word meaning 'Big Village'.

Chicago - Next to Warsaw, Chicago has the largest Polish population in the world.

Detroit - Woodward Avenue in Detroit, Michigan, carries the designation M-1, So named because it was the first paved road anywhere.

Damascus, Syria - was flourishing 2000 years before Rome was founded in 753 BC, making it the oldest continuously inhabited city in existence.

Istanbul, Turkey - is the only city in the world, located on two continents.

Los Angeles - full name is: El Pueblo de Nuestra Senora la Reina de Los Angeles de Porciuncula-- and can be abbreviated to 3.63% of its size: L.A.

New York City - The term 'The Big Apple' was coined by touring jazz musicians of the 1930s who used the slang expression 'apple' for any town or city. Therefore, to play New York City is to play the big time - The Big Apple.

There are more Irish in New York City than in Dublin, Ireland; More Italians in New York City than in Rome, Italy; And more Jews in New York City than in Tel Aviv, Israel.

Ohio - There are no natural lakes in the state of Ohio. Every one is manmade.
Pitcairn Island - The smallest island with country status is Pitcairn
in Polynesia, at just 1.75 sq.Miles/4,53 sq. Km.
Rome - The first city to reach a population of 1 million people was Rome,
Italy in 133 B.C. There is a city called Rome on every continent.
Siberia - contains more than 25% of the world's forests.
S.M.O.M. - The actual smallest sovereign entity in the world is the
Sovereign Military Order of Malta (S.M.O.M).
It is located in the city of Rome, Italy,
Has an area of two tennis courts and, as of 2001, has a population of 80
-- 20 less people than the Vatican.
It is a sovereign entity under international law, just as the Vatican is.
Sahara Desert - In the Sahara Desert, there is a town named Tidikelt,
Algeria, which did not receive a drop of rain for ten years.
Technically though, the driest place on Earth is in the valleys of the
Antarctic near Ross Island.
There has been no rainfall there for two million years.
Spain - literally means 'the land of rabbits'.
St. Paul, Minnesota - was originally called Pig's Eye after a man named
Pierre 'Pig's Eye' Parrant who set up the first business there.
Roads - Chances that a road is unpaved:
in the U.S.A. = 1%;
in Canada = 75%
Russia - The deepest hole ever drilled by man is the Kola Superdeep
Borehole, in Russia. It reached a depth of 12,261 meters (about 40,226 feet
or 7.62 miles).It was drilled for scientific research and gave up some
unexpected discoveries, one of which was a huge deposit of hydrogen –
so massive that the mud coming from the hole was boiling with it.
United States - The Eisenhower interstate system requires that one mile in
 every five must be straight. These straight sections are usable as airstrips in
times of war or other emergencies.

Subject: Be my husband

Mr. Johnson and his secretary are on a train to Paris. They
are just about to go to sleep when the secretary, who has
the hots for her boss, says in a seductive voice, I'm a little
cold, could I borrow your blanket? The man says how would
you like to be Mrs. Johnson for a while? The secretary
jumps at the chance and begins to get out of bed. Then he
replies, good, then you can get your own damn blanket.

Subject: What a low road home

Two drunks were walking home along the railway tracks. The first drunk says, "There's a hell of a lot of steps here." The second drunk says, "I'll tell you what's worse, this hand rail is bloody low down"

Subject: FW: A Fishing Tale

Four married guys go fishing.

After an hour, the following conversation took place:

First guy: 'You have no idea what I had to do to be able to come out fishing this weekend.

I had to promise my wife that I would paint every room next weekend.'

Second guy: 'That is nothing; I had to promise my wife that I would build her a new deck for the pool.'

Third guy: 'Man, you both have it easy! I had to promise my wife that I would remodel the kitchen for her.'

They continue to fish. When they realized that the fourth guy has not said a word, they asked him.

'You haven't said anything about what you had to do to be able to come fishing this weekend.   What's the deal?'

Fourth guy: 'I just set my alarm for 5:30 am.

When it went off, I shut off my alarm, gave the wife a slap on her butt and said:

'Fishing or Sex?' and she said: 'Wear sun-block.'

Subject: What causes *arthritis*

Jock was returning home from the pub, smelling like a distillery.

He flopped on a bus seat next to a priest. His tie was stained; his face was plastered with red lipstick, and a half empty bottle of whiskey was sticking out of his torn coat pocket. He opened his newspaper and began reading. Then he asked the priest, "Father, what causes arthritis?"

"Well my son, it's the result of loose living, being with cheap, wicked women, too much whisky and contempt for your fellow man."

"Well I'll be damned!" Jock muttered, returning to his paper.

The priest, feeling a little guilty, said, "I'm very sorry. I didn't mean to upset you. How long have you had arthritis?"

"I don't, Father. But I was just reading here that the Pope does.

Subject: Library Opening Times

"What time does the library open?" the man on the phone asked.

"Nine am" came the reply.

"And what's the idea of calling me at home in the middle of the night to ask a question like that?"

"Not until nine am.?" the man asked in a disappointed voice.

"No, not till nine am.!" the librarian said. "Why do you want to get in before nine am.?"

"Who said I wanted to get in?" the man sighed sadly. "I want to get out."

Many years ago in Scotland , a new game was invented. It was ruled 'Gentlemen Only...Ladies Forbidden'.. and thus, the word GOLF entered into the English language.

Subject: JUST CALL ME MUM

A young man shopping in a supermarket noticed a little old lady following him around.

If he stopped, she stopped.

Furthermore she kept staring at him.

She finally overtook him at the checkout, and she turned to him and said,

"I hope I haven't made you feel ill at ease;

it's just that you look so much like my late son."

He answered, "That's okay."

"I know it's silly, but if you'd call out "Good bye, Mum" as I leave the store, it would make me feel so happy."

She then went through the checkout, and as she was on her way out of the store, the man called out, "Goodbye, Mum."

The little old lady waved, and smiled back at him.

Pleased that he had brought a little sunshine into someone's day, he went to pay for his groceries.

"That comes to $121.85," said the operator.

"How come so much ... I only bought 5 items..."

The operator replied, "Yeah, but your Mother said you'd be paying for her things."

Don't trust little Old Ladies!!!

I drive way too fast to worry about my cholesterol

Great simplicity is only won by an intense moment or by years of intelligent effort. T.S Eliot

Subject: Hypnotist

Woman comes home and tells her husband, 'Remember those headaches I've been having all these years? Well, they're gone.'
'No more headaches?' the husband asks, 'What happened?'
His wife replies, 'Margie referred me to a hypnotist & he told me to stand in front of a mirror, stare at myself and repeat,
' I do not have a headache '
' I do not have a headache '
' I do not have a headache '
Well, it worked! The headaches are all gone.'
Well, that's wonderful' proclaims the husband.
His wife then says, 'You know, you haven't been exactly a ball of fire in the bedroom these last few years, why don't you go see the hypnotist and see if he can do anything for that? '
Reluctantly, the husband agrees to try it.
Following his appointment, the husband comes home, rips off his clothes, picks up his wife and carries her into the bedroom. He throws her on the bed and says, 'Don't move, I'll be right back.'
He goes into the bathroom and comes back a few minutes later and jumps into bed and makes passionate love to his wife like never before.
His wife says, 'WOW! - that was wonderful!'
The husband says, 'Don't move! I will be right back.'
He goes back into the bathroom, comes back and round two was even better than the first time.
The wife sits up and her head is spinning ' OH MY GOD ' She proclaims.
Her husband again says, 'Don't move, I'll be right back.'
With that, he goes back in the bathroom.
This time, his wife quietly follows him and there, in the bathroom, she sees him standing at the mirror and saying.
'She's not my wife "she's not my wife "she's not my wife "She's not my wife '
His funeral service will be held on Saturday

A 3–legged dog walks into a saloon in the Old Wild West. He slides up to the bar and says: "I'm looking for the man who shot me paw."

Subject: FAMOUS DRINKING QUOTES

WARNING: The consumption of alcohol may cause you to think you can sing.

"I feel sorry for people who don't drink. When they wake up in the morning, that's as good as they're going to feel all day. "

~Frank Sinatra

"When I read about the evils of drinking, I gave up reading."

~ Henny Youngman

"24 hours in a day, 24 beers in a case. Coincidence? I think not."

~ Stephen Wright

"Sometimes when I reflect back on all the wine I drink I feel shame. Then I look into the glass and think about the workers in the vineyards and all of their hopes and dreams. If I didn't drink this wine, they might be out of work and their dreams would be shattered. Then I say to myself, "It is better that I drink this wine and let their dreams come true than be selfish and worry about my liver."

~ Jack Handy

Subject: Wait a few minutes

A policeman was patrolling a local parking spot overlooking a golf course. He drove by a car and saw a couple inside with the dome light on. There was a young man in the driver's seat reading a computer magazine and a young lady in the back seat knitting. He stopped to investigate. He walked up to the driver's window and knocked. The young man looked up, cranked the window down, and said, "Yes Officer?"

"What are you doing?" the policeman asked. "What does it look like?" answered the young man. "I'm reading this magazine." Pointing towards the young lady in the back seat, the officer then asked, "And what is she doing?" The young man looked over his shoulder and replied, "What does it look like? She's knitting."

"And how old are you?" the officer then asked the young man. "I'm nineteen," he replied. "And how old is she?" asked the officer. The young man looked at his watch and said, "Well, in about twelve minutes she'll be sixteen."

Subject: Definitions by gender

REMOTE CONTROL (ri-moht kon-trohl) n.

Female: A device for changing from one TV channel to another.

Male: A device for scanning through all 75 channels every 2 min.

Subject: The Wooden Bowl

I guarantee you will remember the tale of the Wooden Bowl tomorrow, a week from now, a month from now, a year from now.

A frail old man went to live with his son, daughter-in-law, and four-year-old grandson.

The old man's hands trembled, his eyesight was blurred, and his step faltered.

The family ate together at the table. But the elderly grandfather's shaky hands and failing sight made eating difficult. Peas rolled off his spoon onto the floor.

When he grasped the glass, milk spilled on the tablecloth.

The son and daughter-in-law became irritated with the mess.

'We must do something about father,' said the son.

'I've had enough of his spilled milk, noisy eating, and food on the floor.'

So the husband and wife set a small table in the corner.

There, Grandfather ate alone while the rest of the family enjoyed dinner.

Since Grandfather had broken a dish or two, his food was served in a wooden bowl.

When the family glanced in Grandfather's direction, sometimes he had a tear in his eye as he sat alone.

Still, the only words the couple had for him were sharp admonitions when he dropped a fork or spilled food.

The four-year-old watched it all in silence.

One evening before supper, the father noticed his son playing with wood scraps on the floor.

He asked the child sweetly, 'What are you making?' Just as sweetly, the boy responded,

'Oh, I am making a bowl for you and Mama to eat your food in when I grow up. 'The four-year-old smiled and went back to work.

The words so struck the parents so that they were speechless. Then tears

152

started to stream down their cheeks. Though no word was spoken, both knew what must be done.

That evening the husband took Grandfather's hand and gently led him back to the family table.

For the remainder of his days he ate every meal with the family. And for some reason, neither husband nor wife seemed to care any longer when a fork was dropped, milk spilled, or the tablecloth soiled.

On a positive note, I've learned that, no matter what happens, how bad it seems today, life does go on, and it will be better tomorrow.

I've learned that you can tell a lot about a person by the way he/she handles four things:

A rainy day, the elderly, lost luggage, and tangled Christmas tree lights.

I've learned that making a 'living' is not the same thing as making a 'life...'

I've learned that life sometimes gives you a second chance.

I've learned that you shouldn't go through life with a catcher's mitt on both hands. You need to be able to throw something back sometimes.

I've learned that if you pursue happiness, it will elude you

But, if you focus on your family, your friends, the needs of others, your work and doing the very best you can, happiness will find you

I've learned that whenever I decide something with an open heart, I usually make the right decision.

I've learned that even when I have pains, I don't have to be one.

I've learned that every day, you should reach out and touch someone.

People love that human touch — holding hands, a warm hug, or just a friendly pat on the back.

I've learned that I still have a lot to learn.

Subject: How Fights Start

My wife sat down on the settee next to me as I was flipping channels.
She asked, 'What's on TV?'   I said, 'Dust.'
And then the fight started...

****

My wife and I were watching "Who Wants To Be A Millionaire" while we were in bed. I turned to her and said, "Do you want to have sex?"
"No," she answered. I then said, "Is that your final answer?"
She didn't even look at me this time, simply saying, "Yes."
So I said, "Then I'd like to phone a friend."
And then the fight started....

****

Saturday morning I got up early, quietly dressed, made my lunch, and slipped quietly into the garage. I hooked up the boat up to the van, and proceeded to back out into a torrential downpour. The wind was blowing 50 mph, so I pulled back into the garage, turned on the radio, and discovered that the weather would be bad all day. I went back into the house, quietly undressed, and slipped back into bed. I cuddled up to my wife's back, now with a different anticipation, and whispered, "The weather out there is terrible." My loving wife of 5 years replied, "Can you believe my stupid husband is out fishing in that?"
And then the fight started....

****

I rear-ended a car this morning. So, there we were alongside the road and slowly the other driver got out of his car. You know how sometimes you just get sooooo stressed and little things just seem funny? Yeah, well I couldn't believe it.... He was a DWARF!!! He stormed over to my car, looked up at me, and shouted, "I AM NOT HAPPY!!!"
So, I looked down at him and said, "Well, then which one are you?"
And then the fight started.....

****

My wife and I were sitting at a table at my school reunion, and I kept staring at a drunken lady swigging her drink as she sat alone at a nearby table.
My wife asked, 'Do you know her?'
'Yes,' I sighed, 'she's my old girlfriend. I understand she took to drinking right after we split up those many years ago, and I hear she hasn't been sober since.'
'My God!' says my wife, 'who would think a person could be celebrating that long?'
And then the fight started...

****

A woman was standing nude, looking in the bedroom mirror. She was not happy with what she saw and said to her husband, "I feel horrible; I look old, fat and ugly. I really need you to pay me a compliment.'
The husband replied, 'Your eyesight's damn near perfect.'
And then the fight started.....

One year, I decided to buy my mother-in-law a cemetery plot as a Christmas gift...
The next year, I didn't buy her a gift.
When she asked me why, I replied,
"Well, you still haven't used the gift I bought you last year!"
And that's how the fight started

****

After retiring, I went to the Social Security office to apply for Social Security.
The woman behind the counter asked me for my driver's License to verify my age.
I looked in my pockets and realized I had left my wallet at home.
I told the woman that I was very sorry, but I would have to go home and come back later.
The woman said, 'Unbutton your shirt'.
So I opened my shirt revealing my curly silver hair.
She said, 'That silver hair on your chest is proof enough for me' and she processed my Social Security application.
When I got home, I excitedly told my wife about my experience at the Social Security office...
She said, 'You should have dropped your pants. You might have gotten disability, too.'
And then the fight started.

****

When I got home last night, my wife demanded that I take her some place expensive... so, I took her to a gas station.
And then the fight started...

****

To the people who've got an iPhone: you just bought one, you didn't invent it!

In the 1400's a law was set forth in England that a man was allowed to beat his wife with a stick no thicker than his thumb.
Hence we have 'the rule of thumb'

Mickey goes to the judge after speaking to him before about getting a divorce with Minney. The judge says "I'm sorry Mickey but I couldn't find grounds for divorce for being insane. Mickey looks stunned and says
"I didn't say she was insane I said she was fuc**** Goofy

A couple is lying in bed. The man says, "I am going to make you the happiest woman in the world"
The woman says, "I'll miss you."

155

Found in the Cave after the death of Bin Laden

Subject: The Cave (do not distribute outside the Organization)

AL QAIDA - OFFICE OF OSAMA BIN LADEN

CAVE 7422, TORA BORA, AFGANISTAN

Hi guys. We've all been putting in long hours recently but we've really come together as a group and I love that! However, while we continue to fight the infidels in this New Year, we can't forget to take care of the cave, and frankly I have a few concerns.

First of all, while it's good to be concerned about cruise missiles, we should be even more concerned about the dust in our cave. We want to avoid excessive dust inhalation (a health and safety issue), so we need to sweep the cave daily. I've done my bit on the cleaning – rota. Have you? I've posted a sign-up sheet near the cave reception area (next to the halal toaster).

Second, it's not often I make a video address. But when I do, I'm trying to scare the shit out of most of the world's population, okay? That means that while we're taping, please do not ride your scooter in the background or keep doing the 'wassup' thing. Thanks.

Third - food. I bought a box of Dairylea recently. I clearly wrote "Ossy" on the front, and put it on the top shelf. Today, two of my Dairylea slices were gone. Consideration - that's all I'm saying.

Fourth, I'm not against team spirit and all that, but we must distance ourselves from the infidel's bat and ball games. Please do not chant "Ozzy, ozzy, ozzy, oi, oi, oi" when I ride past on the donkey. Thanks.

Fifth - graffiti. Whoever wrote "OSAMA F**KS DONKEYS" on the group toilet wall - it's a lie. The donkey backed into me, whilst I was relieving myself at the edge of the mountain.

Sixth, the use of chickens is strictly for food. The old excuse that the 'chicken backed into me, whilst I was relieving myself at the edge of the mountain' will not be accepted in future (with donkeys, there is a grey area).

Finally, we've heard that there may be Western soldiers in disguise trying to infiltrate our ranks. I want to set up patrols to look for them. First patrol will be Omar, Muhammad, Abdul, Akbar and Dave.

Love you lots,

Group Hug.

Os.

PS - I'm sick of having "Osama Bed Linen" scribbled on my laundry bag. Cut it out, it's not funny anymore.

Better to remain silent and be thought a fool, than to speak and remove all doubt.

A seal walks into a bar and asks the bartender for a drink.
The bartender asks the seal, "What's your pleasure?"
The seal replies, "Anything but a Canadian Club."

Subject: Blonde and Redhead friend

Two friends, a blonde and a redhead, are walking down the street and pass a flower shop where the redhead happens to see her boyfriend buying flowers.
She sighs and says, "Oh, crap, my boyfriend is buying me flowers again." The blonde looks quizzically at her and says, "You don't like getting flowers?"
The redhead says, "I love getting flowers, but he always has expectations after giving me flowers, and I just don't feel like spending the next three days on my back with my legs in the air."
The blonde says, "Don't you have a vase?"

Subject: Need Samples

An old man goes to the doctor for his yearly physical, his wife tagging along.
When the doctor enters the examination room, he tells the old man, "I need a urine sample, a stool sample and a sperm sample."
The old man, being hard of hearing, looks at his wife and yells: "WHAT?"
"What did he say? What's he want?"
His wife yells back, "He needs your underwear."

I wondered why the Frisbee was getting bigger, and then it hit me.

What happens if you get scared half to death twice?

I went to my allotment last week and found someone had covered it with 2 inches of soil. I went again yesterday only to find it covered again with another 2 inches of soil.
The plot thickens!!!

A friend of mine moved into a new house at the weekend so I took him over a couple of radiators.
Just a little house warming present.

Subject: Saturday night bath

It was time for Father John's Saturday night bath and the new young nun, Sister Magdalene, had prepared the bath water and towels just the way the old nun had instructed.

Sister Magdalene was also instructed not to look at Father John's nakedness if she could help it, do whatever he told her to do, and pray.

The next morning the old nun asked Sister Magdalene how the Saturday night bath had gone.

'Oh, sister,' said the young nun dreamily, 'I've been saved.' 'Saved? And how did that come about?' asked the old nun.

'Well, when Father John was soaking in the tub, he asked me to wash him, and while I was washing him he guided my hand down between his legs where he said the Lord keeps the Key to Heaven.'

'Did he now?' said the old nun evenly.

Sister Magdalene continued, 'And Father John said that if the Key to Heaven fits my lock, the portals of Heaven would be opened to me and I would be assured salvation and eternal peace. And then Father John guided his Key to Heaven into my lock.'

'Is that a fact?' said the old nun even more evenly.

'At first it hurt terribly, but Father John said the pathway to salvation was often painful and that the glory of God would soon swell my heart with ecstasy. It did, it felt so good being saved.'

'That wicked old bastard' said the old nun.

'He told me it was Gabriel's Horn, and I've been blowing it for 40 years.'

If a statue in the park of a person on a horse has both front legs in the air, the person died in battle. If the horse has one front leg in the air, the person died because of wounds received in battle. If the horse has all four legs on the ground, the person died of natural causes

HUSBAND: Shall we try a different position tonight?
WIFE: That's a good idea... you stand by the ironing board while I sit on the sofa and fart.

Spelling has bekum a loost art.

Nelson Mandela

Nelson Mandela is sitting at home watching TV and drinking a beer when he hears a knock at the door. When he opens it, he is confronted by a little Chinese man, clutching a clip board and yelling, 'You Sign! You sign!' Behind him is an enormous truck full of car exhausts.

Nelson is standing there in complete amazement, when the Chinese man starts to yell louder, 'You Sign! You sign!'

Nelson says to him, 'Look, you've obviously got the wrong man', and shuts the door in his face.

The next day he hears a knock at the door again. When he opens it, the little Chinese man is back with a huge truck of brake pads. He thrusts his clipboard under Nelson's nose, yelling, 'You sign! You sign!'

Mr Mandela is getting a bit hacked off by now, so he pushes the little Chinese man back, shouting: 'Look, go away! You've got the wrong man. I don't want them!' Then he slams the door in his face again.

The following day, Nelson is resting, and late in the afternoon, he hears a knock on the door again. On opening the door, there is the same little Chinese man thrusting a clipboard under his nose, shouting, 'You sign! You sign!' Behind him are TWO very large trucks full of car parts.

This time Nelson loses his temper completely, he picks up the little Man by his shirt front and yells at him: 'Look, I don't want these! Do you understand? You must have the wrong name! Who do you want to give these to?'

The little Chinese man looks very puzzled, consults his clipboard, and says:

'You not **Nissan Main Deala?'**

If you ain't makin' waves, you ain't kickin' hard enough!

My girlfriend told me that she was seeing another man. I told her to rub her eyes.
Emo Philips

Man who leaps off cliff, jumps to conclusion

Subject: THE EFFICIENCY EXPERT

An efficiency expert concluded his lecture with a note of caution. "You don't want to try these techniques at home." "Why not?" asked somebody from the back.
"I watched my wife's routine at breakfast for years," the expert explained.
"She made lots of trips between the refrigerator, stove, table and cabinets, often carrying a single item at a time.
One day I told her, 'Hon, why don't you try carrying several things at once?'"
"Did it save time?" the person in the audience asked.
"Actually, yes," replied the expert.
"It used to take her 20 minutes to make breakfast.
Now I do it in seven."

Subject: Police warning - BEER

Police are warning all men who frequent clubs, parties & local pubs to be alert and stay cautious when offered a drink by any woman.
Many females use a date-rape-drug on the market called **' Beer'**.
The drug is found in liquid form and is available anywhere.
It comes in bottles, cans, or from taps and in large kegs.
Beer is used by female sexual predators at parties and bars to persuade their male victims to go home and sleep with them.
A woman needs only to get a guy to consume a few units of **Beer** and then simply ask him home for no-strings-attached sex.
Men are rendered helpless against this approach.
After several **Beers,** men will often succumb to the desires to sleep with horrific looking women to whom they would never normally be attracted.
After drinking **Beer ,** men often awaken with only hazy memories of exactly what happened to them the night before, often with just a vague feeling that 'something bad' occurred.
At other times these unfortunate men are swindled out of their life's savings, in a familiar scam known as **'a relationship'**. In extreme cases, the female may even be shrewd enough to entrap the unsuspecting male into a longer-term form of servitude and punishment referred to as **'marriage'.**
Men are much more susceptible to this scam after **Beer** is administered and sex is offered by the predatory females.
Please forward this warning to every male you know.
If you fall victim to this **' Beer'** scam and the women administering it, there are male support groups where you can discuss the details of your shocking encounter with similarly victimized men.
For the support group nearest you, just look up **'Golf Courses'** in the phone book.

Subject: Keeping myself pure

This guy in a bar notices a woman, always alone, who comes in on a fairly regular basis. After the second week, he made his move.

"No thank you," she said politely." "This may sound rather odd in this day and age, but I'm keeping myself pure until I meet the man I love."

"That must be rather difficult," the man replied.

"Oh, I don't mind too much," she said. "But, it has my husband pretty upset."

Subject: Keep this philosophy in mind the next time you hear, or are about to repeat a rumour.

Socrates

In ancient Greece (469 - 399 BC), Socrates was widely lauded for his wisdom. One day the great philosopher came upon an acquaintance, who ran up to him excitedly and said, "Socrates, do you know what I just heard about one of your students...?"

"Wait a moment," Socrates replied. "Before you tell me, I'd like you to pass a little test. It's called the Test of Three."

"Test of Three?" "That's correct," Socrates continued.

"Before you talk to me about my student, let's take a moment to test what you're going to say.

The first test is Truth. Have you made absolutely sure that what you are about to tell me is true?"

"No," the man replied, "actually I just heard about it."

"All right," said Socrates. "So you don't really know if it's true or not. Now let's try the second test, the test of Goodness. Is what you are about to tell me about my student something good?"

"No, on the contrary..."

"So," Socrates continued, "you want to tell me something bad about him even though you're not certain it's true?"

The man shrugged, a little embarrassed.

Socrates continued, "You may still pass though because there is a third test - the filter of Usefulness. Is what you want to tell me about my student going to be useful to me?""No, not really..."

"Well," concluded Socrates, "if what you want to tell me is neither True nor Good nor even Useful, why tell it to me at all?"

The man was defeated and ashamed and said no more.

This is the reason Socrates was a great philosopher and held in such high esteem.

It also explains why Socrates never found out that Plato was banging his wife.

Subject: FWD WHAT'S UP

Lovers of the English language enjoy this. It is an example of why people learning English have trouble. Learning the nuances of English makes it a difficult language.

This two-letter word in English has more meanings than any other two-letter word, and that word is 'UP.'

It is listed in the dictionary as an [adv], [prep], and [adj], [n] or [v].

It's easy to understand UP, meaning toward the sky or at the top of the list, but when we awaken in the morning, why do we wake UP?

At a meeting, why does a topic come UP? Why do we speak UP, and why are the officers UP for election and why is it UP to the secretary to write UP a report? We call UP our friends, brighten UP a room, polish UP the silver, warm UP the leftovers and clean UP the kitchen. We lock UP the house and fix UP the old car.

At other times this little word has real special meaning.

People stir UP trouble, line UP for tickets, work UP an appetite, and think UP excuses.

To be dressed is one thing but to be dressed UP is special.

And this UP is confusing: A drain must be opened UP because it is stopped UP.

We open UP a store in the morning but we close it UP at night. We seem to be pretty mixed UP about UP!

To be knowledge able about the proper uses of UP, look UP the word UP in the dictionary. In a desk-sized dictionary, it takes UP almost ¼ of the page and can add UP to about thirty definitions

If you are UP to it, you might try building UP a list of the many ways UP is used. It will take UP a lot of your time, but if you don't give UP, you may wind UP with a hundred or more.

When it threatens to rain, we say it is clouding UP. When the sun comes out we say it is clearing UP. When it rains, it soaks UP the earth. When it does not rain for awhile, things dry UP. One could go on & on, but I'll wrap it UP, for now ....my time is UP!

Oh...one more thing:

What is the first thing you do in the morning & the last thing you do at night?

U   P!

Now I'll shut UP

162

Subject: More Quotes

Men are simple things. They can survive a whole weekend with only three things: beer, boxer shorts and batteries for the remote control.
~ **Diana Jordan** ~

All men are not homeless, but some men are home less than others.
~ **Henry Youngman** ~

DUMB BLONDE

A blonde teenager, wanting to earn some extra money for the summer, decided to hire herself out as a 'handy-woman' and started canvassing a nearby well-to-do neighbourhood. She went to the front door of the first house, and asked the owner if he had any odd jobs for her to do. 'Well, I guess I could use somebody to paint my porch,' he said,
'How much will you charge me?' Delighted, the girl quickly responded,
'How about $50?' The man agreed and told her that the paint brushes and everything she would need was in the garage. The man's wife, hearing the conversation said to her husband, 'Does she realize that our porch goes ALL the way around the house?' He responded, 'That's a bit cynical, isn't it?' The wife replied, ' You're right. I guess I'm starting to believe all those dumb blonde jokes we've been getting by e-mail lately.'
Later that day, the blonde came to the door to collect her money.
'You're finished already?' the startled Husband asked.
'Yes, the blonde replied, and I even had paint left over, so I gave it two coats.'
Impressed, the man reached into his pocket for the $50 and handed it to her along with a ten dollar tip. 'And by the way, ' the blonde added,
'It's not a Porch, it's a Lexus.'

Subject: The Airline Pilot

A plane was taking off from Mascot (Sydney) Airport. After it reached a comfortable cruising altitude, the captain made an announcement over the intercom, 'Ladies and gentlemen, this is your captain speaking. Welcome to Flight Number XYZ, non-stop from Sydney to Auckland. The weather ahead is good and, therefore, we should have smooth and uneventful flight. Now sit back and relax - ARGHHH! OH, MY GOD!' Silence followed and after a few minutes, the captain came back on the intercom and said, 'Ladies and Gentlemen, I am so sorry if I scared you earlier, but, while I was talking, the flight attendant brought me a cup of coffee and spilled the hot coffee in my lap. You should see the front of my pants!' A passenger in Economy said, 'That's nothing. He should see the back of mine!'

Jack Benny is walking down the street, when a stick-up man pulls out a gun and says "Your money or your life!" An extremely long silence follows. "Your money or your life!" the thug repeats. Finally Benny says "Hang on, I'm thinking.

Subject: AADD- KNOW THE SYMPTOMS.....

Recently, I was diagnosed with A.A.A.D.D. -
(Age Activated Attention Deficit Disorder.)

This is how it manifests itself:

I decide to water my garden. As I turn on the hose in the driveway, I look over at my car and decide it needs washing.

As I head towards the garage, I notice post on the porch table that I picked up from the postman earlier. I decide to go through it before I wash the car. I put my car keys on the table, put the junk mail in the recycling box under the table, and notice that the recycling box is full.

So, I decide to put the bills back on the table and take out the recycling first. But then I think, since I'm going to be near the post box when I take out the recycling paper anyway, I may as well pay the bills first. I take my cheque book off the table and notice that there is only one cheque left.

My extra cheques are in the desk in my study, so I go into the house to my desk where I find the cup of coffee I'd been drinking.

I'm going to look for my cheques but first I need to push the coffee aside so that I don't accidentally knock it over. The coffee is getting cold, and I decide to make another cup. As I head toward the kitchen with the cold coffee, a vase of flowers on the worktop catches my eye - the flowers need water. I put the coffee on the worktop and discover my reading glasses that I've been searching for all morning. I decide I better put them back on my desk, but first I'm going to water the flowers.

I put the glasses back down on the worktop, fill a container with water and suddenly spot the TV remote control. Someone left it on the kitchen table. I realise that tonight when we go to watch TV, I'll be looking for the remote, but I won't remember that it's on the kitchen table, so I decide to put it back where it belongs, but first I'll water the flowers.

I pour some water in the flowers, but quite a bit of it spills on the floor.

So, I put the remote back on the table, get some towels and wipe up the spill. Then, I head down the hall trying to remember what I was planning to do.

At the end of the day:

The car isn't washed. The bills aren't paid

There is a cold cup of coffee sitting on the kitchen work-surface

The flowers don't have enough water,

There is still only 1 cheque in my cheque book,

I can't find the remote, I can't find my glasses,

And I don't remember what I did with the car keys.

Then, when I try to figure out why nothing got done today, I'm really baffled because I know I was busy all bloody day and I'm really tired.

I realise this is a serious problem, and I'll try to get some help for it, but first I'll check my e-mails.....

THIS IS A NONPARTISAN JOKE THAT CAN BE ENJOYED BY All PARTIES!
NOT ONLY THAT-- IT IS POLITICALLY CORRECT!!

While walking down the street one day a "Member of Parliament" was tragically hit by a truck and died.

His soul arrived in heaven and was met by St. Peter at the entrance.

'Welcome to heaven,' said St. Peter. 'Before you settle in, it seems there is a problem. We seldom see a high official around these parts you see, so we're not sure what to do with you.'

'No problem, just let me in,' said the man.

'Well, I'd like to, but I have orders from higher up. What we'll do is have you spend one day in hell and one in heaven. Then you can choose where to spend eternity.'

'Really, I've made up my mind. I want to be in heaven,' said the MP.

'I'm sorry, but we have our rules.'

And with that, St. Peter escorted him to the elevator and he was sent down, down, down to hell. The doors opened and he found himself in the middle of a green golf course. In the distance was a clubhouse, standing in front of it were all his deceased friends, many of whom were politicians who had worked with him.

Everyone was very happy and in evening dress. They ran to greet him, shaking his hand, and reminiscing about the good times they had while getting rich at the expense of the people.

They play a friendly game of golf and then dine on lobster, caviar and champagne.

Also present is the devil, who really is a very friendly & nice guy who enjoyed dancing and telling jokes. They are having such a good time that before he realized it, it was time to go.

The M.P. received a hearty farewell and waved while the elevator began to move upwards...

The elevator went up, up, up and the door reopened in heaven where St. Peter was waiting for him.

'Now it's time to visit heaven.'

So, 24 hours pass with the M.P. joining a group of contented souls moving from cloud to cloud, playing their harps and singing. They had a good time and, before he realized it, the 24 hours had gone by and St. Peter returned.

'Well, then, you've spent a day in hell and another in heaven. Now choose your eternity.'

The MP reflects for a minute, then he answers: 'Well, I would never have said it before, I mean heaven has been delightful, but I think I would be better off in hell.'

So St. Peter escorts him to the elevator and he went down, down, down to hell.

The doors of the elevator opened and he's in the middle of a barren land covered with waste and garbage.

He saw all his friends, dressed in rags, picking up the trash and putting it in black bags as more trash fell from above.

The devil came over to him and put an arm around his shoulders. 'I don't understand,' stammered the M.P. 'Yesterday I was here and there was a golf course and clubhouse, and we ate lobster and caviar, drank champagne, and danced and had a great time... Now there's just a wasteland full of garbage and my friends look miserable. What happened?'

The devil looked at him, smiled and said,
'Yesterday we were campaigning...
Today you voted.'

Subject: Where is your husband?

One day three women were at a beauty parlour talking about their husbands. The first woman says, "Last night my husband said he was going to his office, but when I called they said he wasn't there!"

"I know!" the next woman says, "Last night my husband said he was going to his brother's house but when I called he wasn't there."

The third woman says, "I always know where my husband is."

"Impossible!" both women say, "He has you completely fooled!"

"Oh no," says the woman. "I'm a widow."

Subject: LIVE FOR TODAY

A friend of mine opened his wife's underwear drawer and picked up a silk paper wrapped package:
'This, - he said - isn't any ordinary package.'
He unwrapped the box and stared at both the silk paper and the box.
'She got this the first time we went to New York, 8 or 9 years ago. She has never put it on, was saving it for a special occasion.
Well, I guess this is it.
He got near the bed and placed the gift box next to the other clothing he was taking to the funeral house. His wife had just died.
He turned to me and said:
'Never save something for a special occasion.
Every day in your life is a special occasion'.
I still think those words changed my life.
Now I read more and clean less.
I sit on the porch without worrying about anything.
I spend more time with my family, and less at work.
I understood that life should be a source of experience to be lived up to, not survived through.
I no longer keep anything. I use crystal glasses every day.
I'll wear new clothes to go to the supermarket, if I feel like it.
I don't save my special perfume for special occasions; I use it whenever I want to.
The words 'Someday' and 'One Day' are fading away from my dictionary.
If it's worth seeing, listening to or doing, I want to see, listen or do it **now**...don't know what my friend's wife would have done if she knew she wouldn't be there the next morning, this nobody can tell.
I think she might have called her relatives and closest friends.
She might call old friends to make peace over past quarrels.
I'd like to think she would go out for Chinese, her favourite food.
It's these small things that I would regret not doing, if I knew my time had come.
Each day, each hour, each minute, is special.
Live for today, for tomorrow is promised to no-one.

Subject: What do you want

If you want happiness for an hour, take a nap.
If you want happiness for a day, go fishing.
If you want happiness for a year, inherit a fortune.
If you want happiness for a lifetime, help somebody. (Chinese proverb)

Is there another word for synonym?

Subject: An Obituary printed in the London Times – Interesting and sadly rather true.

Today we mourn the passing of a beloved old friend, **Common Sense**, who has been with us for many years. No one knows for sure how old he was, since his birth records were long ago lost in bureaucratic red tape. He will be remembered as having cultivated such valuable lessons as:

- Knowing when to come in out of the rain;
- Why the early bird gets the worm;
- Life isn't always fair;
- and maybe it **was** my fault.

Common Sense lived by simple, sound financial policies (don't spend more than you can earn) and reliable strategies (adults, not children, are in charge).

His health began to deteriorate rapidly when well-intentioned but overbearing regulations were set in place. Reports of a 6-year-old boy charged with sexual harassment for kissing a classmate; teens suspended from school for using mouthwash after lunch; and a teacher fired for reprimanding an unruly student, only worsened his condition.

Common Sense lost ground when parents attacked teachers for doing the job that they themselves had failed to do in disciplining their unruly children.

It declined even further when schools were required to get parental consent to administer sun lotion or an aspirin to a student; but could not inform parents when a student became pregnant and wanted to have an abortion.

Common Sense lost the will to live as the churches became businesses; and criminals received better treatment than their victims.

Common Sense took a beating when you couldn't defend yourself from a burglar in your own home and the burglar could sue you for assault.

Common Sense finally gave up the will to live, after a woman failed to realize that a steaming cup of coffee was hot. She spilled a little in her lap, and was promptly awarded a huge settlement, against the restaurant.

Common Sense was preceded in death, by his parents, Truth and Trust, by his wife, Discretion, by his daughter, Responsibility, and by his son, Reason.

He is survived by his 4 stepbrothers;

I Know My Rights

I Want It Now

Someone Else Is To Blame

I'm A Victim

Not many attended his funeral because so few realized he was gone. If you still remember him, pass this on. If not, join the majority and do nothing.

Subject: LITTLE GIRL'S DOG

A little girl asks her mum, 'Mum, can I take Lulu for a walk around the block?'
Her mum replies 'No, because she is on heat.'
'What does that mean?' asked the child.
'Go and ask your father. I think he's in the garage.'
The little girl goes out to the garage and says, 'Dad, can I take Lulu for a walk around the block? I asked Mum, but she said Lulu was on the heat, and to come ask you.'
He took a rag, soaked it in petrol, and scrubbed the dog's backside with it to disguise the scent, and said 'Ok, you can go now, but keep Lulu on the leash and only go once around the block.'
The little girl left and returned a few minutes later with no dog on the leash...
Surprised, Dad asked, 'Where's Lulu?
'The little girl said, 'She ran out of petrol about halfway round the block, so another dog is pushing her home.'

Very few people can afford to be poor.

Where there's a will, there's an Inheritance Tax.

Make love, not war.   Hell, do both - get married!
Women's restroom

Subject: Thomas Jefferson was a very remarkable man who started learning very early in life and never stopped.

At 5, began studying under his cousin's tutor.

At 9, studied Latin, Greek and French.

At 14, studied classical literature and additional languages.

At 16, entered the College of William and Mary.

At 19, studied Law for 5 years starting under George Wythe.

At 23, started his own law practice.

At 25, was elected to the Virginia House of Burgesses.

At 31, wrote the widely circulated "Summary View of the Rights of British America" and retired from his law practice.

At 32, was a Delegate to the Second Continental Congress.

At 33, wrote the Declaration of Independence.

At 33, took three years to revise Virginia's legal code and wrote a Public Education bill and a statute for Religious Freedom.

At 36, was elected the second Governor of Virginia succeeding Patrick Henry.

At 40, served in Congress for two years.

At 41, was the American minister to France and negotiated commercial treaties with European nations along with Ben Franklin and John Adams.

At 46, served as the first Secretary of State under George Washington.

At 53, served as Vice President and was elected president of the American Philosophical Society.

At 55, drafted the Kentucky Resolutions and became the active head of Republican Party.

At 57, was elected the third president of the United States.

At 60, obtained the Louisiana Purchase doubling the nation's size.

At 61, was elected to a second term as President.

At 65, retired to Monticello.

At 80, helped President Monroe shape the Monroe Doctrine.

At 81, almost single-handedly created the University of Virginia and served as its first president.

At 83, died on the 50th anniversary of the Signing of the Declaration of Independence.

Thomas Jefferson knew how to succeed because he himself studied the previous failed attempts at government. He understood actual history, the nature of God, his laws and the nature of man. That happens to be way more than what most understand today. Jefferson really knew his stuff. A voice from the past to lead us in the future:

John F. Kennedy held a dinner in the white House for a group of the brightest minds in the nation at that time. He made this statement: "This is perhaps the assembly of the most intelligence ever to gather at one time in the White House with the exception of when Thomas Jefferson dined alone."

When we get piled upon one another in large cities, as in Europe, we shall become as corrupt as Europe.

Thomas Jefferson

The democracy will cease to exist when you take away from those who are willing to work and give to those who would not.
Thomas Jefferson

It is incumbent on every generation to pay its own debts as it goes. A principle which if acted on would save one-half the wars of the world.
Thomas Jefferson

I predict future happiness for Americans if they can prevent the government from wasting the labours of the people under the pretence of taking care of them.
Thomas Jefferson

My reading of history convinces me that most bad government results from too much government.
Thomas Jefferson

No free man shall ever be debarred the use of arms.
Thomas Jefferson

The strongest reason for the people to retain the right to keep and bear arms is, as a last resort, to protect themselves against tyranny in government.
Thomas Jefferson

The tree of liberty must be refreshed from time to time with the blood of patriots and tyrants.
Thomas Jefferson

To compel a man to subsidize with his taxes the propagation of ideas which he disbelieves and abhors is sinful and tyrannical.
Thomas Jefferson

Thomas Jefferson said in 1802:
I believe that banking institutions are more dangerous to our liberties than standing armies. If the American people ever allow private banks to control the issue of their currency, first by inflation, then by deflation, the banks and corporations that will grow up around the banks will deprive the people of all property - until their children wake-up homeless on the continent their fathers conquered. (How true this has turned out to be.)

What do you get when you pour cement on a burglar?
A hardened criminal.

What's the difference between a woman with PMS and a Pitt Bull?
Lipstick

Subject: The Gay Flight Attendant

My flight was being served by an obviously gay flight attendant, who seemed to put everyone in a good mood as he served us food and drinks. As the plane prepared to descend, he came swishing down the aisle and told us "Captain Marvey has asked me to announce that he'll be landing the big scary plane shortly, so lovely people, if you could just put your trays up, that would be super."

On his trip back up the aisle, he noticed this well-dressed and rather Arabic looking woman hadn't moved a muscle.

"Perhaps you didn't hear me over those big brute engines but I asked you to raise your trazy-poo, so the main man can pitty-pat us on the ground."

She calmly turned her head and said, "In my country, I am called a Princess and I take orders from no one."

To which the flight attendant replied, without missing a beat, "Well, sweet-cheeks, in my country I'm called a Queen so I outrank you.

So put the tray-up, Bitch"

Subject: Three men were hiking through a forest...

When they came upon a large raging, violent river.
Needing to get to the other side, the first man prayed:
'God, please give me the strength to cross the river.
Poof!!!
God gave him big arms and strong legs...
And he was able to swim across in about 2 hours,
Having almost drowned twice.
After witnessing that, the second man prayed:
'God, please give me strength and the tools to cross the river'
Poof!!!
God gave him a rowboat and strong arms and strong legs...
And he was able to row across In about an hour
After almost capsizing once
Seeing what happened to the first two men, The third man prayed:
'God, please give me the strength, the tools and the intelligence to cross the river'
Poof!!!
HE WAS TURNED INTO A WOMAN!!!
She checked the map, hiked one hundred yards upstream...
And walked across the bridge

A passionate kiss, like a spider's web, leads to undoing of fly.

Subject: TOP TEN THINGS ONLY WOMEN UNDERSTAND
10. Cats' facial expressions.
9. The need for the same style of shoes in different colours.
8. Why bean sprouts aren't just weeds.
7. Fat clothes.
6. Taking a car trip without trying to beat your best time.
5. The difference between beige, ecru, cream, off-white, and eggshell.
4. Cutting your hair to make it grow.
3. Eyelash curlers.
2. The inaccuracy of every bathroom scale ever made.
AND, the Number One thing only women understand:
OTHER WOMEN

Subject: Pregnancy, Oestrogen, and Women
PREGNANCY Q & A & more!

Q: Should I have a baby after 35?
A: No, 35 children is enough.
Q: I'm two months pregnant now. When will my baby move?
A: With any luck, right after he finishes university.
Q: What is the most reliable method to determine a baby's sex?
A: Childbirth.
Q: My wife is five months pregnant and so moody that sometimes she's borderline irrational.
A: So what's your question?
Q: My childbirth instructor says it's not pain I'll feel during labour, but pressure. Is she right?
A: Yes, in the same way that a cyclone might be called an air current.
Q: When is the best time to get an epidural?
A: Right after you find out you're pregnant.
Q: Is there any reason I have to be in the delivery room while my wife is in labour?
A: Not unless the word 'child support payment' means anything to you.
Q: Is there anything I should avoid while recovering from childbirth?
A: Yes, pregnancy.
Q: Do I have to have a baby shower?
A: Not if you change the baby's nappy very quickly
Q: Our baby was born last week. When will my wife begin to feel and act normal again?
A: When the kids are in university.

Subject: The Fire Truck

A fire fighter was working on the engine outside the Station, when he noticed a little girl nearby in a little red wagon with little ladders hung off the sides and a garden hose tightly coiled in the middle.

The girl was wearing a fire fighter's helmet.

The wagon was being pulled by her dog and her cat.

The fire fighter walked over to take a closer look.

'That sure is a nice fire truck,' the fire fighter said with admiration.

'Thanks,' the girl replied. The fire fighter looked a little closer. The girl had tied the wagon to her dog's collar and to the cat's testicles.

'Little partner,' the fire fighter said, 'I don't want to tell you how to run your rig, but if you were to tie that rope around the cat's collar, I think you could go faster. '

The little girl replied thoughtfully, 'You're probably right, but then I wouldn't have a siren.'

Subject: 'OESTROGEN ISSUES'

10 WAYS TO KNOW IF YOU HAVE 'OESTROGEN ISSUES'

1. Everyone around you has an attitude problem.
2. You're adding chocolate chips to your cheese omelette.
3. The dryer has shrunk every last pair of your jeans.
4. Your husband is suddenly agreeing to everything you say.
5. You're using your mobile phone to dial up every bumper sticker that says: 'How's my driving-call 0800-'.
6. Everyone's head looks like an invitation to batting practice.
7. Everyone seems to have just landed here from 'outer space.'
9. You're sure that everyone is scheming to drive you crazy.
10. The Nurofen Plus box is empty and you bought it yesterday.

Subject: Grandma's Great Idea

A man was walking down the street when he noticed his grandpa sitting on the porch, in the rocking chair, with nothing on from the waist down.

"Grandpa, what are you doing?" he exclaimed. The old man looked off in the distance and didn't answer him. "Grandpa, what are you doing sitting out here with nothing on below the waist?" he asked again.

The old man slyly looked at him and said, "Well, last week I sat out here with no shirt on, and I got a stiff neck. This was your Grandma's idea!"

Subject: Answered Prayer

The pastor asked if anyone in the congregation would like to express Praise for answered prayers. A lady stood and walked to the podium. She said, "I have Praise. Two months ago, my husband, Tom, had a terrible bicycle accident and his scrotum was completely crushed. The pain was excruciating and the doctors didn't know if they could help him."

You could hear a muffled gasp from the men in the congregation as they imagined the pain that poor Tom must have experienced.

"Tom was unable to hold me or the children," she went on "and every move caused him terrible pain. We prayed as the doctors performed a delicate operation, and it turned out they were able to piece together the crushed remnants of Tom's scrotum, and wrap wire around it to hold it in place."

Again, the men in the congregation were unnerved and squirmed uncomfortably as they imagined the horrible surgery performed on Tom.

"Now," she announced in a quavering voice, "thank the Lord, Tom is out of the hospital and the doctors say with time, his scrotum should recover completely." All the men sighed with relief. The pastor rose and tentatively asked if anyone else had something to say.

A man stood up and walked slowly to the podium.

He said, "I'm Tom.

The entire congregation held its breath.

"I just want to tell my wife that the word is Sternum."

Subject: THE TRUSTING WIFE

There comes a time when a woman just has to trust her husband... for example...

A wife comes home late at night and quietly opens the door to her bedroom.

From under the blanket she sees four legs instead of two. She reaches for a cricket bat and starts hitting the blanket as hard as she can.

Once she's done, she goes to the kitchen to have a drink.

As she enters, she sees her husband there, reading a magazine. "Hi Darling", he says, "Your parents have come to visit us, so I let them stay in our bedroom. Did you say 'hello'?"

Lady who goes camping must beware of evil intent.

Minds are like Parachutes. They work best when open.

Subject: What Love means to a 4-8 year old.

A group of professional people posed this question to a group of 4 to 8 year olds, 'What does love mean?'
The answers they got were broader and deeper than anyone could have imagined. See what you think:

'When my grandmother got arthritis, she couldn't bend over and paint her toenails anymore.
So my grandfather does it for her all the time, even when his hands got arthritis too. That's love.'
Rebecca- age 8

'When someone loves you, the way they say your name is different.
You just know that your name is safe in their mouth.'
Billy - age 4

'Love is when a girl puts on perfume and a boy puts on shaving cologne and they go out and smell each other.'
Karl - age 5

'Love is when you go out to eat and give somebody most of your French fries without making them give you any of theirs.'
Chrissy - age 6

'Love is what makes you smile when you're tired.'
Terri - age 4

'Love is when my mommy makes coffee for my daddy and she takes a sip before giving it to him, to make sure the taste is OK.'
Danny - age 7

'Love is when you kiss all the time. Then when you get tired of kissing, you still want to be together and you talk more.
My Mommy and Daddy are like that. They look gross when they kiss'
Emily - age 8

'Love is what's in the room with you at Christmas if you stop opening presents and listen.'
Bobby - age 7 (Wow!)

'If you want to learn to love, you should start with a friend who you hate,'
Nikka - age 6
(we need a few million more Nikka's on this planet)

'Love is when you tell a guy you like his shirt, then he wears it every day'
Noelle - age 7

'Love is like a little old woman and a little old man who are still friends even after they know each other so well.'
Tommy - age 6

'During my piano recital, I was on a stage and I was scared. I looked at all the people watching me and saw my daddy waving and smiling.
He was the only one doing that. I wasn't scared anymore.'
Cindy - age 8

'My mommy loves me more than anybody
You don't see anyone else kissing me to sleep at night.'
Clare - age 6

'Love is when Mommy gives Daddy the best piece of chicken.'
Elaine-age 5

'Love is when Mommy sees Daddy smelly and sweaty and still says he is handsomer than Robert Redford.'
Chris - age 7

'Love is when your puppy licks your face even after you left him alone all day.'
Mary Ann - age 4

'I know my older sister loves me because she gives me all her old clothes and has to go out and buy new ones.'
Lauren - age 4

'When you love somebody, your eyelashes go up and down and little stars come out of you.' (what an image)
Karen - age 7

'Love is when Mommy sees Daddy on the toilet and she doesn't think it's gross.'
Mark - age 6

'You really shouldn't say 'I love you' unless you mean it. But if you mean it, you should say it a lot. People forget.'
Jessica - age 8

And the final one
The winner was a four year old child whose next door neighbour was an elderly gentleman who had recently lost his wife.
Upon seeing the man cry, the little boy went into the old gentleman's yard, climbed onto his lap, and just sat there.
When his Mother asked what he had said to the neighbour, the little boy said,
'Nothing, I just helped him cry'

Subject: The Verdict

The DA stared at the jury, unable to believe the "not guilty" verdict he'd just heard.
Bitterly, he asked, "What possible excuse could you have for acquitting this man?"
The foreman answered, "Insanity."
The attorney responded, still incredulous, "I could understand that. . .
But- all twelve of you?"

SPECIAL ID BADGE

The other day I needed to go to the local NHS hospital but not wanting to sit there for 4 hours, I put on my blue jacket and pinned on a plastic ID card that I had made off the Internet onto the front of my jacket.

When I went into the hospital, I noticed that three quarters of the people got up and left. I guess they decided that they weren't that sick after all. Cut at least 3 hours off my waiting time.

Feel free to use it the next time you're in need of quicker emergency service. It also works at all supermarkets. It saves me hours.

At the Laundry, three minutes after entering, I had my choice of any machine, most still running!

Don't try it at McDonald's though.. The whole staff disappeared and I never got my order !!!!!

Also......... never wear it while trying to get a taxi !!

Here's the patch.

Subject: HEAVEN OR HELL

A man and his dog were walking along a road. The man was enjoying the scenery, when it suddenly occurred to him that he was dead.

He remembered dying, and that the dog walking beside him had been dead for years. He wondered where the road was leading them.

After a while, they came to a high, white stone wall along one side of the road. It looked like fine marble... At the top of a long hill, it was broken by a tall arch that glowed in the sunlight.

When he was standing before it he saw a magnificent gate in the arch that looked like mother-of-pearl, and the street that led to the gate looked like pure gold. He and the dog walked toward the gate, and as he got closer, he saw a man at a desk to one side.

When he was close enough, he called out, 'Excuse me, where are we?' 'This is Heaven, sir,' the man answered.

'Wow! Would you happen to have some water?' the man asked.

Of course, sir. Come right in, and I'll have some ice water brought right up. 'The man gestured, and the gate began to open.

'Can my friend,' pointing toward his dog, 'come in, too?' he asked.

'I'm sorry, sir, but we don't accept pets.'

The man thought a moment and then turned back toward the road and continued the way he had been going with his dog.

After another long walk, and at the top of another long hill, he came to a dirt road leading through a farm gate that looked as if it had never been closed. There was no fence.

As he approached the gate, he saw a man inside, leaning against a tree and reading a book.

'Excuse me!' he called to the man. 'Do you have any water?'

'Yeah, sure, there's a pump over there, come on in.'

'How about my friend here?' the traveller gestured to the dog.

'There should be a bowl by the pump.'

They went through the gate, and sure enough, there was an old-fashioned hand pump with a bowl beside it.

The traveller filled the water bowl and took a long drink himself, then he gave some to the dog.

When they were full, he and the dog walked back toward the man who was standing by the tree..

'What do you call this place?' the traveller asked.

'This is Heaven,' he answered.

'Well, that's confusing,' the traveller said. 'The man down the road said that was Heaven, too.'

'Oh, you mean the place with the gold street and pearly gates? Nope. That's hell.'

'Doesn't it make you mad for them to use your name like that?'

'No, we're just happy that they screen out the folks who would leave their best friends behind.'

What is the one thing that unites all men, regardless of gender, race, religion, economic status, or ethnic background?

Deep down inside, we ALL believe that we are superb drivers.

War does not determine who is right, it determines who is left.

Marriage is the process of finding out what kind of man your wife would have preferred.

A bus is a vehicle that runs twice as fast when you are after it as when you are in it.

Better to be pissed off than pissed on.

It takes many nails to build a crib, but one screw to fill it.

Man who drives like hell is bound to get there.

Each king in a deck of playing cards represents a great king from history:

Spades - King David

Hearts - Charlemagne

Clubs -Alexander, the Great

Diamonds - Julius Caesar

Subject: THE LAWS OF ULTIMATE REALITY

Law of Mechanical Repair

After your hands become coated with grease, your nose will itch and you have to pee.

Law of Gravity

Any tool, when dropped, will roll to the least accessible corner.

Law of Probability

The probability of being watched is directly proportional to the stupidity of your act.

Law of Random Numbers

If you dial a wrong number, you never get a busy signal and someone always answers.

Law of the Alibi

If you tell the boss you were late for work because you had a flat tyre, the very next morning you will have a flat tyre.

Variation Law

If you change lines (or traffic lanes), the one you were in will always move faster than the one you are in now (works every time).

Law of the Bath

When the body is fully immersed in water, the telephone rings.

Law of Close Encounters

The probability of meeting someone you know increases dramatically when you are with someone you don't want to be seen with.

Law of the Result

When you try to prove to someone that a machine won't work, it will.

Law of Biomechanics

The severity of the itch is inversely proportional to the reach.

Law of the Theatre

At any event, the people whose seats are furthest from the aisle arrive last.

Murphy's Law of Lockers

If there are only two people in a locker room, they will have adjacent lockers.

Law of Logical Argument

Anything is possible if you don't know what you are talking about.

Law of Physical Surfaces

The chances of an open-faced jelly sandwich landing face down on a floor covering are directly correlated to the newness and cost of the carpet/rug.

Brown's Law of Physical Appearance

If the shoe fits, it's ugly.

Oliver's Law of Public Speaking

A closed mouth gathers no feet.

Wilson 's Law of Commercial Marketing Strategy

As soon as you find a product that you really like, they will stop making it.

Subject: The Drunk

A man walks into the front door of a bar. He is obviously drunk. He staggers up to the bar, seats himself on a stool, and with a belch, asks the bartender for a drink.

The bartender politely informs the man that it appears that he has already had plenty to drink; he could not be served additional liquor at this bar but could get a cab called for him. The drunk is briefly surprised then softly scoffs, grumbles, climbs down off the bar stool, and staggers out the front door.

A few minutes later, the same drunk stumbles in the side door of the bar. He wobbles up to the bar and hollers for a drink. The bartender comes over, and still politely, but more firmly refuses to serve the man due to his inebriation. Again, the bartender offers to call a cab for him. The drunk looks at the bartender for a moment angrily, curses, and shows himself out the side door, all the while grumbling and shaking his head.

A few minutes later, the same drunk bursts in through the back door of the bar. He plops himself up on a bar stool, gathers his wits, and belligerently orders a drink.

The bartender comes over and emphatically reminds the man that he is clearly drunk, will be served no drinks, and either a cab or the police will be called immediately.

The surprised drunk looks at the bartender and in hopeless anguish, cries "Man! How many bars do you work at?"

Subject: Keep it Silent

I was in the restaurant yesterday when I suddenly realized I desperately needed to pass gas. The music was really, really loud, so I timed my gas with the beat of the music.

After a couple of songs, I started to feel better. I finished my coffee, and noticed that everybody was staring at me....

Then I suddenly remembered that I was listening to my iPod.

Subject: Early suspicion

Adam has been staying out very late for a few nights and Eve becomes quite upset. "What's wrong, darling?" he asks her.

"You're seeing another woman," she replies.

"Eve, darling, you're totally wrong," says Adam. "You know you're the only woman on earth for me."

They continue to argue until Adam falls asleep. But then he is suddenly woken up by a strange pain in his chest. He looks up and sees Eve poking him very vigorously.

"What do you think you're doing?" asks Adam angrily.

"I'm counting your ribs," replies Eve.

182

Subject: The Paper Cowboy

This cowboy walks into a bar and orders a beer. His hat is made of brown wrapping paper. And so are his shirt, vest, chaps, pants, and boots. His spurs are also made of paper. Pretty soon, the sheriff arrives and arrests him for rustling.

Subject: Anyone for Tennis?

Little Billy asks his dad for a telly in his room. Dad reluctantly agrees.
Next day Billy comes downstairs and asks, 'Dad, what's love juice?' Dad looks horrified and tells Billy all about sex. Billy just sat there with his mouth open in amazement. Dad says: 'So what were you watching'?' Billy says, ' Wimbledon'

Q. What do bulletproof vests, fire escapes, windshield wipers and laser printers have in common?
A. All were invented by women.

The Grim Reaper came for me last night, and I beat him off with a vacuum cleaner.
Strewth, talk about Dyson with death.

Q. What is the cheapest time to call your friends long distance?
A. When they're not home!

I live in California, and my watch is three hours fast.
I can't fix it, so I'm moving to New York

Subject: THE LOVING HUSBAND

A man had two of the best tickets around the 18th green for the last day of the Ryder Cup. As he sits down, another man comes along and asks if anyone is sitting in the seat next to him.
"No", he says, "the seat is empty." "This is incredible!" said the man, "who in their right mind would have a seat like this on this occasion, the biggest golfing event of the year & not use it?"
He says, "Well, actually, the seat belongs to me. My wife was supposed to come with me but she passed away. This is the first home based Ryder Cup that we haven't been to together since we got married."
"Oh.....I'm sorry to hear that. That's terrible. I guess you couldn't find someone else, a friend or relative or even a neighbour to take the seat?"
The man shakes his head... "No... They're all at the funeral."

I'm sure wherever my dad is; he's looking down on us.
He's not dead, just very condescending.

Squirrel who runs up woman's' leg will not find nuts.

Two secrets to keep your marriage brimming...
1. Whenever you're wrong, admit it,
2. Whenever you're right, shut up.
- Patrick Murra

Everywhere is within walking distance if you have the time.   - Steven Wright

Subject: Bar Jokes

An Irish man walks into a bar. The bartender looks at him and notices he has a steering wheel stuck down the front of his pants. "Hey," he says, "What's with the steering wheel down your pants?" "Ach," says the Irish man, "it's driving me nuts!"

A guy walks into a bar and orders a drink. After a few more he needs to go to the can. He doesn't want anyone to steal his drink so he puts a sign on it saying, "I spat in this beer, do not drink!". After a few minutes he returns and there is another sign next to his beer saying, "So did I!"

A man walks into a bar with a giraffe and they proceed to get blitzed. The giraffe drinks so much it passes out on the floor. The man gets up and heads for the door to leave when the bartender yells, "Hey! You can't leave that lying there!" The drunk replies, "That's not a lion! It's a giraffe."

Adult: A person who has stopped growing at both ends and is now growing in the middle.

If you want children to keep their feet on the ground, put some responsibility on their shoulders.

The wife has been missing a week now. Police said to prepare for the worst. So I've been to the charity shop to get all her clothes back.

184

Subject: How Microsoft can help

There was a pilot flying a small single engine charter plane, with a couple of very important executives on board. He was coming into Seattle airport through thick fog with less than 10m visibility when his instruments went out. So he began circling around looking for landmark.

After an hour or so, he starts running pretty low on fuel and the passengers are getting very nervous. Finally, a small opening in the fog appears and he sees a tall building with one guy working alone on the fifth floor. The pilot banks the plane around, rolls down the window and shouts to the guy "Hey, where am I? To this, the solitary office worker replies "You're in a plane."

The pilot rolls up the window, executes a 275 degree turn and proceeds to execute a perfect blind landing on the runway 5 miles away. Just as the plane stops, so does the engine as the fuel has run out.

The passengers are amazed and one asks how he did it. "Simple" replies the pilot, "I asked the guy in that building a simple question. The answer he gave me was 100 percent correct, but absolutely useless, therefore that must be Microsoft's support office and from there the airport is 275 degrees and 5 miles away."

Borrow money from pessimists--they don't expect it back

Subject: The Union Plumber

A plumber was called to woman's apartment in New York City to repair a leaking pipe. When he arrived he was pleased to discover that the woman was quite a luscious, well-stacked dish.

During the course of the afternoon, the two became extremely friendly. About 6:30 p.m. the phone rang, disturbing the bedroom shenanigans.

"That was my husband," she said, putting down the phone. "He's on his way home, but is going back to the office around 8 p.m. Come back then, dear, and we can take up where we left off."

The union plumber looked at the woman in disbelief.

"What? On my own time?"

A meeting is a gathering of important people who individually can't do anything but together can decide that nothing can be done

There are only 10 kinds of people that understand binary - those that do, and those that don't.

Ambition is a poor excuse for not having enough sense to be lazy.

The most effective way to remember your wife's birthday is to forget it once.

You know the indestructible black box on aeroplanes. Why don't they make the whole plane out of that stuff?

Man who runs in front of car gets tired, man who runs behind car gets exhausted.

Man who fight with wife all day get no piece at night.

Subject: Fw: Fwd: The Irish!:

Joe says to Paddy: "Close your curtains the next time you're shagging your wife. The whole street was watching and laughing at you yesterday." Paddy says: "Well the joke's on them stupid bastards, because I wasn't even at home yesterday."

Paddy says to Mick - I'm ready for a holiday, only this year I'm going to do it a bit different. 3 years ago I went to Spain and Mary got pregnant. 2 years ago I went to Italy and Mary got pregnant. Last year I went to Majorca and Mary got pregnant. Mick asks - So what are you going to do this year?. Paddy replies, - I'll take her with me!

"Paddy & Mick find three grenades, so they take them to a police station. Mick: "What if one explodes before we get there?" Paddy: "We'll lie and say we only found two."

186

Subject: SHAY

What would you do? You make the choice. Don't look for a punch line, there isn't one. Read it anyway. My question is: Would you have made the same choice?

At a fundraising dinner for a school that serves children with learning disabilities, the father of one of the students delivered a speech that would never be forgotten by all who attended. After extolling the school and its dedicated staff, he offered a question:

'When not interfered with by outside influences, everything nature does, is done with perfection.

Yet my son, Shay, cannot learn things as other children do. He cannot understand things as other children do.

Where is the natural order of things in my son?'

The audience was stilled by the query.

The father continued. 'I believe that when a child like Shay, who was mentally and physically disabled comes into the world, an opportunity to realize true human nature presents itself, and it comes in the way other people treat that child.'

Then he told the following story:

Shay and I had walked past a park where some boys Shay knew were playing baseball. Shay asked, 'Do you think they'll let me play?' I knew that most of the boys would not want someone like Shay on their team, but as a father I also understood that if my son were allowed to play, it would give him a much needed sense of belonging and some confidence to be accepted by others in spite of his handicaps.

I approached one of the boys on the field and asked (not expecting much) if Shay could play. The boy looked around for guidance and said, 'We're losing by six runs and the game is in the eighth inning. I guess he can be on our team and we'll try to put him in to bat in the ninth inning.'

Shay struggled over to the team's bench and, with a broad smile, put on a team shirt. I watched with a small tear in my eye and warmth in my heart. The boys saw my joy at my son being accepted.

In the bottom of the eighth inning, Shay's team scored a few runs but was still behind by three.

In the top of the ninth inning, Shay put on a glove and played in the right field. Even though no hits came his way, he was obviously ecstatic just to be in the game and on the field, grinning from ear to ear as I waved to him from the stands.

In the bottom of the ninth inning, Shay's team scored again.

Now, with two outs and the bases loaded, the potential winning run was on base and Shay was scheduled to be next at bat.

At this juncture, do they let Shay bat and give away their chance to win the game?

Surprisingly, Shay was given the bat. Everyone knew that a hit was all but impossible because Shay didn't even know how to hold the bat properly, much less connect with the ball.

However, as Shay stepped up to the plate, the pitcher, recognizing that the other team was putting winning aside for this moment in Shay's life, moved in a few steps to lob the ball in softly so Shay could at least make contact.

The first pitch came and Shay swung clumsily and missed.

The pitcher again took a few steps forward to toss the ball softly towards Shay.

As the pitch came in, Shay swung at the ball and hit a slow ground ball right back to the pitcher. The game would now be over.

The pitcher picked up the soft grounder and could have easily thrown the ball to the first baseman.

Shay would have been out and that would have been the end of the game..

Instead, the pitcher threw the ball right over the first baseman's head, out of reach of all team mates.

Everyone from the stands and both teams started yelling, 'Shay, run to first! Run to first!'

Never in his life had Shay ever run that far, but he made it to first base.

He scampered down the baseline, wide-eyed and startled.

Everyone yelled, 'Run to second, run to second!'

Catching his breath, Shay awkwardly ran towards second, gleaming and struggling to make it to the base.

By the time Shay rounded towards second base, the right fielder had the ball. The smallest guy on their team who now had his first chance to be the hero for his team.

He could have thrown the ball to the second-baseman for the tag, but he understood the pitcher's intentions so he, too, intentionally threw the ball high and far over the third-baseman's head.

Shay ran toward third base deliriously as the runners ahead of him circled the bases toward home.

All were screaming, 'Shay, Shay, Shay, all the Way Shay'

Shay reached third base because the opposing shortstop ran to help him by turning him in the direction of third base, and shouted, 'Run to third! Shay, run to third!' As Shay rounded third, the boys from both teams, and the spectators, were on their feet screaming, 'Shay, run home! Run home!'

Shay ran to home, stepped on the plate, and was cheered as the hero who hit the grand slam and won the game for his team

'That day', said the father softly with tears now rolling down his face, 'the boys from both teams helped bring a piece of true love and humanity into this world'.

Shay didn't make it to another summer. He died that winter, having never forgotten being the hero and making me so happy, and coming home and seeing his Mother tearfully embrace her little hero of the day!

AND NOW A LITTLE FOOT NOTE TO THIS STORY:

We all send thousands of jokes through the e-mail without a second thought, but when it comes to sending messages about life choices, people hesitate.

The crude, vulgar, and often obscene pass freely through cyberspace, but public discussion about decency is too often suppressed in our schools and workplaces.

If you're thinking about forwarding this message, chances are that you're probably sorting out the people in your address book who aren't the 'appropriate' ones to receive this type of message Well, the person who sent you this, believes that we all can make a difference.

We all have thousands of opportunities every single day to help realize the 'natural order of things.'

So many seemingly trivial interactions between two people present us with a choice:

Do we pass along a little spark of love and humanity or do we pass up those opportunities and leave the world a little bit colder in the process?

A wise man once said every society is judged by how it treats it's least fortunate amongst them.

It was the accepted practice in Babylon 4,000 years ago that for a month after the wedding, the bride's father would supply his son-in-law with all the mead he could drink. Mead is a honey beer and because their calendar was lunar based, this period was called the honey month, which we know today as the honeymoon.

```
They've opened a new shop across the road selling
camouflage clothing but I have my suspicions something
weird is going on.
Yesterday I saw 20 people go in but I never saw anyone
coming out.
```

When a man steals your wife, there is no better revenge than to let him keep her.

Q.. If you were to spell out numbers, how far would you have to go until you would find the letter 'A'?

A. One thousand

Subject: Fw: God.com

Dear Lord,

1. Every single evening
As I'm lying here in bed,
This tiny little Prayer
Keeps running through my head:

2. God bless all my family
Wherever they may be,
Keep them warm
And safe from harm
For they're so close to me.

3. And God, there is one more thing
I wish that you could do;
Hope you don't mind me asking,
Please bless my computer too.

4. Now I know that it's unusual
To Bless a motherboard,
But listen just a second
While I explain it to you, Lord...

5. You see, that little metal box
Holds more than odds and ends;
Inside those small compartments
Rest so many of my friends.

6. I know so much about them
By the kindness that they give,
And this little scrap of metal
Takes me in to where they live.

7. By faith is how I know them
Much the same as you.
We share in what life brings us
And from that our friendships grew.

8. Please take an extra minute
From your duties up above,
To bless those in my address book
That's filled with so much love.

9. Wherever else this prayer may reach
To each and every friend,
Bless each e-mail inbox
And each person who hits 'send'.

I intend to live forever – so far, so good

FINALLY SOME POINTS TO PONDER

Would a fly without wings be called a walk?

What is the speed of dark?

Which **is** the other side of the street?

If you wait to have kids until you can afford them, you probably never will.

It is impossible to lick your own elbow.

What WAS the best thing **before** sliced bread?

Why does your nose run, and your feet smell?

Better to understand a little than to misunderstand a lot.

And finally, finally

First you must build a tunnel before you can see light at the end of it.

References:
1. *Hooker –rugby football playing position.*
2. *Ryanair – Dublin based Low Fare Airline – thought by some to be rude at times.*
3. *Liverpool – N.W England Soccer Team.*
4. *Harrods – Large, expensive, departmental store in London*
5. *Shoeing – Pun on shooing as putting shoes on horses and shooing; term used to get an animal to leave.*
6. *Sainsbury's – Large UK Supermarket.*
7. Et's foo ae coo's shite an pish – Scottish dialect for 'full of cow's piss and shite.
8. Coronation Street – British Soap Opera
9. Boot – Trunk.
10. Tesco – UK's largest supermarket.
11. Martin McGuinness – N Ireland Nationalist Politician.
12. Newcastle-Upon-Tyne – N. E. England city.
13. Bishoploch Primary School – Glasgow, Scotland primary school.
14. Cherie Blair – Wife of the UK's ex Prime Minister, Tony Blair.
15. Greenock – A famous shipbuilding area near Glasgow.
16. Nancy Astor - became the first woman MP to take her seat in the UK House of Commons.
17. Disraeli – 19th century British Prime Minister.
18. Walter Kerr – US Theatre Critic.
19. Clarence Darrow – US Lawyer & Writer.
20. William Faulkner – US writer and Nobel Laureate.
21. Moses Hadas –US Teacher, translator, scholar, and rabbi.
22. Stephen Bishop – Musician & Singer.
23. Samuel Johnson – 18th century English literature writer most famous for his publication of *A Dictionary of the English Language* (1755)
24. Irvin S Cobb - was an American author, humorist, and columnist.
25. Charles, Count Talleyrand – 19th century French diplomat and statesman.
26. Paul Keating - is a British actor from London, England.
27. Forrest Tucker - was an American actor in both movies and television from the 1940s to the 1980s.
28. Andrew Lang - was a Scots poet, novelist, and literary critic.
29. Billy Wilder - was an Austro-Hungarian born American filmmaker, screenwriter, producer, artist, and journalist, whose career spanned more than 50 years and 60 films.